LOST IN THOUGHT

LOST IN
THOUGHT

The Hidden
Pleasures of an
Intellectual Life

ZENA HITZ

PRINCETON UNIVERSITY PRESS

PRINCETON AND OXFORD

Published by Princeton University Press
41 William Street, Princeton, New Jersey 08540
6 Oxford Street, Woodstock, Oxfordshire OX20 1TR

press.princeton.edu

ISBN 978-0-691-17871-4
ISBN (e-book) 978-0-691-18923-9

British Library Cataloging-in-Publication Data is available

Editorial: Rob Tempio and Matt Rohal
Production Editorial: Jenny Wolkowicki
Text design: Leslie Flis
Jacket design: Matt Avery / Monograph
Production: Danielle Amatucci
Publicity: Jodi Price and Amy Stewart
Copyeditor: Maia Vaswani

Jacket art: iStock

This book has been composed in Arno Pro text with DIN 1451 Engschrift
display

Printed on acid-free paper. ∞

Printed in the United States of America

10 9 8 7 6 5 4 3 2 1

They all ate, and were satisfied. Luke 9:17

For my brothers and our parents

CONTENTS

Prologue

HOW WASHING DISHES RESTORED MY INTELLECTUAL LIFE

כִּי-טוֹבָה חָכְמָה מִפְּנִינִים וְכָל-חֲפָצִים לֹא יִשְׁווּ-בָהּ:

For wisdom is better than rubies;
> And all that you may desire cannot compare with her.
> —PROVERBS 8:11[1]

Midway through the journey of my life, I found myself in the woods of eastern Ontario, living in a remote Catholic religious community called Madonna House. We lived by a river that froze into flat, icy landscapes in the winter, giving off mist as it thawed and froze again. In summer the water warmed to allow swimming or boat trips through thick weeds up into the wild and empty vistas of the river valley. Our manner of life was rustic, as poor as it was hidden, thanks to the community's deliberate commitment to poverty. We slept in dormitories, used water sparingly, wore donated clothing, and ate vegetables either in the short growing season or as the root cellar or the freezer permitted.

The work varied and was assigned under obedience. I was the baker for a time, stewarding the capricious yeast and the fire of the oven, emerging at the end of the day covered in dough, flour, and ash. I then worked in the handicrafts department, restoring furniture, repairing books, organizing materials, decorating for holidays. I joked that I was being trained as a nineteenth-century housewife. Next, I was assigned to the library; then to a long stint cleaning and researching donated antiques for the community's gift shop. I shared in the common work of housecleaning and washing dishes, as well as planting, weeding, and harvesting vegetables. As in many such communities, we switched jobs often enough that no one could be fully identified with their work. This made it easier to see work not as a vehicle for achievement but as a form of service: talent and interest were valuable but ultimately irrelevant. Certainly, neither any of these "jobs" nor the basic approach to life was what I had spent the previous twenty years preparing for. From the age of seventeen until I left for Canada at the age of thirty-eight, I had been dedicated full time to institutions of higher learning, first as a student and then as a professor and a scholar of classical philosophy.

My life as a professional intellectual had its roots in my childhood. From my earliest memory I lived with books of all kinds. There were stacks on my bedroom floor and they lined the dusty walls of our Victorian house. My older brother taught me to read and infected me with an appetite for reading; my parents were both lovers of books, words, and ideas without professional training or support, amateurs in the original and best sense. San Francisco in the 1970s was a strange place for many famous reasons, but its basic commitment to leisure is clear to me only now that we have passed into a far less leisurely age. Reading and thinking for their own sake went along with outings to the stony beaches or dark mountain forests of Northern California, without a clear object or specialized skills or expensive equipment. The standard for success of an activity was enjoying oneself in fellowship with others; such endeavors included the arts and crafts projects that no one would ever buy, and musical performances whose value would evaporate at too great a distance from the campfire.

That natural foods were superior to processed ones was a hard fact to swallow—I needed threats and wheedling to be induced to consume carob or brewer's yeast or foul-tasting medicinal tea. But I required no convincing to find that learning was a joy. My family was fond of fierce arguments over matters of fact, when no one present knew what they were talking about: world records and body counts, the proper classification of living things, and the nature of a lunar eclipse. The dictionary, the encyclopedia, and the almanac were the final reference points by which the arguments were settled. These resolutions were never entirely satisfactory. In the reference books we found ammunition for yet further discussion and argument. Not one piece of knowledge that we sought or acquired was useful for any purpose whatsoever.

My brother and I pursued obsessions with wild animals, especially sea creatures. We knew all seventeen species of penguin and the feeding habits of whales. Large, blubbery sea lions sometimes surfaced at the local seashore; otherwise, we relied on books or visits to the local science museum, studying our beloved objects through whale skeletons or at the thick-glassed dolphin tank that replayed recorded dolphin sounds when we pressed a button at the side. We amassed a vast collection of stuffed animals, who formed a political community and elected a small walrus as president. We established a constitution for them, wrote civic anthems, and, of course, told stories. We imagined our way into the lives of animals, fusing animal and human capacities as children have always done.

Larger questions lurked unexpressed behind our sea of facts and our playful imagining. What is a human being? Is it enough to see, feel, eat, swim, squeak? Are we a part of nature, or somehow outside of nature? My father and I once discussed that question, sitting on a rock in a mountain stream on a camping trip, in the shade of clustered redwoods. It seemed unimaginable that we were like the forest, running water, or rock around us. Somehow a human being stands outside of the natural, and yet even a child knows that the time will come when breath is gone and all is overcome by weight, resistance, decay, and fermentation, our flesh traveling through the gullets of animals to become dirt and slime and dust.

My family did not undertake intellectual practices and concerns as a means to an end. They did not consider them to be preparation for life, but rather a way of spending one's time that had its worth in itself. Accordingly, they did not blink when I left home to study old books and fundamental human questions at a tiny liberal arts college on the East Coast, a secular school under the improbable religious name of St. John's College. My parents did not ask me what use I would find the study of epic poems or ancient treatises on plants, whether it would help me to find my way in the world. Not that my choice was foreordained: my brother, for instance, pursued specialized training in biochemistry. But I needed neither prodding nor reassurance to study the liberal arts. The value of such an education, as one path among others, was simply obvious to us.

This first phase of my academic life began in spectacular growth and excitement. I loved my little college at first sight: the willows at the water's edge; the green lawn sloping down to them, suited for summer rolling and winter sledding; the colonial redbrick buildings that both charmed and startled me, fresh as I was from brick-free earthquake country. I was instantly at ease in the bare-bones classrooms, each furnished with only a large wooden table, old-fashioned caned chairs, and wraparound blackboards. Our classes proceeded without agendas, the discussion driven by the living questions that we and our teachers brought to the room. Accordingly, our conversations could flounder in indifference or lack of preparation; they could chug along steadily, building quiet momentum; or they could explode with the excitement of a newly discovered insight. I was enchanted by the honesty of the project: as the books were, as the questions were, as the human beings who participated were, so the discussion went. There was no artificial clarity or forced organization to soften the discomfort of the work of the mind, no cushion between us and the difficulties or dangers of inquiry or the thrill of discovery.

Our seminars met in the evening and spilled over into discussion on the steps, on the quad, at the bar. A formal lecture on Friday evenings was followed by a question period of indefinite length, in which a good topic and a lively conversation might lead us past midnight and into the early morning—leaving the speaker an exhausted wreck, but the students fired up for more. (These nocturnal practices continue today, but I speak in the past, when I first encountered them.)

We all assumed that books mattered for life, but we knew so little about life that our earnest musings must have sounded ridiculous to any mature ear. Every book was connected with every other; the slightest technical detail in grammar or geometry was full of romance and significance that it would be gauche to articulate clearly. We loved the feeling of insight, but were inexperienced in the thing itself. Still, as if to will our maturity into being, our teachers spoke to us as if our ideas mattered and so treated us as free adults, capable of making significant choices and coming to our own decisions about the hardest questions.

In mathematics and science our forms of inquiry were especially unconventional and exciting. We studied what mathematicians and scientists wrote and tried out what they practiced or experimented. We then saw scientific and mathematical thinking as a human endeavor rather than a body of established facts to be memorized or a prefabricated skill that had been determined as necessary by nameless and faceless authorities. Mathematical and scientific skills, it turns out, are developed as means to ends, as routes to understanding, solutions to practical problems, or vehicles of contemplation, and they are as various as forms of play or styles of fine art. The "established facts" were neither: they were boiled-down versions of tentative truths that would be partly preserved, partly destroyed in the next generation of theory.

I blossomed in the simplicity and spontaneity of life at the college: the exclusive focus on reading and conversation, the insistence on asking basic human questions, the conviction that the value of intellectual activity lay in the search more than the achievement. I remember writing an essay on *Oedipus Rex* as a freshman and being overwhelmed with the delight of discovering new (to me) insights. I walked about in the pale green of spring trees in rapt distraction, thinking about things, and I knew that, somehow, I had found an essential piece of my future life.

———

After graduation, many of my classmates took their supposedly useless liberal arts education out of the ivory tower and into the realms of politics, law, business, journalism, and nonprofit initiatives. They founded schools and peopled law firms, corporate boards, the *New York Times*, international nongovernmental organizations, and high reaches of the US government. They found, in other words, that study for its own sake—that is, study without visible results or high-prestige credentials—was enormously useful for other ends. I ended up through a series of lucky breaks in the world of elite academia, where—after some initial struggle—I too was very successful. But my eventual success planted the seeds for long years of gradual and crushing disillusionment with academic life.

At first, graduate school was also tremendously exciting. I learned the ancient professional trades that underlie the great books and their confrontation with human questions: scholarship, commentary, and interpretation. By custom, my colleagues in classical philosophy, faculty and graduate students, gathered into informal reading groups whenever we found ourselves in sufficient numbers. As we sat around a table with an ancient text in front of us, sharing our puzzles with one another and tossing out ideas, I found the intellectual honesty and spontaneity of my undergraduate years, while seeing further into the depths and the details. I developed a love for the intricacies of Greek grammar. I found my way into library work, still one of my greatest pleasures: I chased sources, references, and associations through the fluorescent-lit labyrinths of the stacks, stumbling into strange corners, certain to discover something either illuminating or hilarious, or both. I learned the delightful mental gymnastics of analytic philosophy, in which any manner of thesis whatsoever is defended, explored, and almost always refuted. I understood that our scattered communities of scholars and teachers were part of a grand international and transhistorical project for the preservation and transmission of learning. I learned over time, first as a graduate student and then as a young professor, that the amateur's human questions are always the best questions for scholars to start from.

I also began a different kind of training in graduate school, bound by invisible but powerful threads to the first sort. From the casual conversation of my teachers and fellow students, I learned how to navigate the byzantine social hierarchy of the academic world. I learned whom to admire, and whom to disdain.

To be told who was "out" made one feel included in the "in"—but, of course, the ruthlessness and ubiquity of the practice of judgment suggested how fragile my own limited success was. Through hearing scorn pronounced on academic failure and rejection, and through pronouncing it myself, I developed a terror of being judged wanting by my teachers and my peers. Like many graduate students, I learned to obsessively scan the behavior of others for signs of increased or lost favor. Like virtually all of them, I was convinced that I alone was in danger of failure, and everyone else was sailing through with perfect confidence.

The fear of failure had a flip side, of course: an intense desire to succeed at the game of prestige, to prove myself as good as some and better than others. I had a very vivid and strange dream early on in graduate school, a dream unlike any I've had before or since. I dreamed that one of my teachers, whom I admired very much and on whose approval I depended, was leading a seminar on the topic of niceness, dressed in his academic gown. (The dreamworld has its peculiarities: the seminar took place in my high-school gym, with the addition of a grand escalator.) In the dream I asked him why he cared about being nice, given his stratospheric academic prestige. He turned to me in horror, took me by the arm, led me out of the room, and questioned me as to what I meant. When I repeated myself, he said to me with great emphasis: "I care about niceness, I do, very much. I want to be loved . . . adored . . ."—his voice dropped to a dramatic whisper—". . . *worshipped.*"

The dream was, of course, very amusing to me and to my fellow students, to whom I immediately related it. But it contained a fundamental insight that my conscious life could not bear, an insight perhaps into my teacher in particular but more certainly into the values of academic life in general—at least in some departments, and at least as I lived it. To say we sought status and approval sounds more bloodless than it was: we wanted it at the expense of others. We observed and cultivated, for instance, the thrill of the critical academic takedown, a ritual act of humiliation that usually took place in public. A cutting book review, a devastating objection from the back of the lecture hall: these were a currency of success, not despite but because of their cruelty. We viewed such events with awe, as if to tacitly recognize their inhuman character. Our embrace of public acts of competitive humiliation mixed in a sickly way with our perception of the real loftiness of learning. The victors in these gladiatorial contests thus took on a certain grandeur that inspired fascination and idolatry. And this idolatry, elsewhere recognized as celebrity, was what we wanted for ourselves. That was simply what mattered to us—or rather, to those of us, like myself, who lacked a sufficient inner core of humanity to defend against it.

It must be said that I threw myself into brutal competition for status and prestige without much thought and with few conscious misgivings. I lacked at first the professional skills and habits I needed to move comfortably, but before long I was swimming like a fish in water, as much at home in the gossip-sea as in the library stacks. It helped that the waters were not always easy to tell apart. Our energetic expressions of superiority might mix seamlessly with a philosophical conversation that lasted until sunrise; we went home, slept, and took it up again. It took a number of years before the invisible thread in me that bound the drama of reputation to the steady, serious process of real learning began to become undone, unwinding the rest of my life along with it.

By 2001 I had been a graduate student for five years at three different universities. (I took a master's at the first, and transferred from the second.) By then the initial struggles and shocks were far behind, and I was luxuriating in academic success, in an environment bursting with intellectual life and with friends with whom any conversation was possible. The twin plants of intellectual joy and of achievement in prestige and status had grown together so closely that, to me, their blossoming was indistinguishable, each from the other. One morning in September, I walked as usual onto campus via one of its tree-lined paths. As I walked, one of the department staff called out something to me about a dramatic news story and I stopped into the student center to look at a television. When I arrived, the live image of the World Trade Center, each tower in flames, was on the screen. I sat down and read the tickers from the bottom of the screen, trying to put the pieces together. A few minutes later, one of the towers collapsed into ash. The announcers on the news immediately lost their words.

During a lab experiment in college, I was once accidentally exposed to a large charge of static electricity. It was as if everything stopped and started again, as if someone had hit my reset button, or as if I were an Etch A Sketch whose elaborate patterns had been suddenly shaken to a gray blank. The moment that the first tower collapsed was much like that. Everything in me stopped. Out of the shocked blankness came the insistent thought that I had to quit philosophy and *do something*, to break out of the world of the library and into the world of action and international affairs—a world that I imagined in ignorance, knowing only slogans and catchphrases.

The bombings immediately took on a national meaning, one that I drank in without thinking much on it. It was easy at that time to believe in the exceptional nature of the event, in the specialness of the victims, and so I did. But the nationalist impulse was a reduction of the real and perceptible effect of the events on me, an unconscious attempt to normalize and contain their unsettling and unearthly character. Along with the news-fueled sorrow came what was for me uncharacteristic kindness. I remember seeing someone drop some file folders on campus and rushing immediately to help, that person's need blotting out everything else—a trivial event, but somehow luminous to me. I was able to see during that time wounds on people's faces: broken, vulnerable looks. I found that I spoke more freely and openly to my friends and family, and they to me. The new forms of awareness and motivation stuck out in my mind. They puzzled me. I remember as they faded, I found myself wishing that something else terrible would happen to renew the effect—and then, of course, recoiling at myself.

It took some months for these uncharacteristically compassionate feelings and impulses to fade, and for my normal self-absorption to reassert itself. But the disenchantment with academic life lasted quite a bit longer. I sensed that I belonged to a broader community of human beings than the community of scholars. What was the point of studying philosophy and classics? What conceivable difference could it make in the face of the suffering world? It did not help that the academic world is famously, and truly, insular. Events and ideas from outside it enter through a narrow and peculiarly shaped gate, so that the experience of them always feels predigested. I longed for a broader experience, to gain my own traction over events in some way.

My tentative explorations of alternate career paths such as human rights work or politics felt so uncomfortable that I knew they would not suit me. Lacking a clear way forward, I decided to press on with my academic career with a simple change of dissertation topic. My old project, an investigation into ancient views of self-knowledge, was now dry as dust to my eyes; I turned to a more "relevant" study of the ancient critiques of democracy.

The crisis unresolved, there formed in me a wide, icy river of discontent that would surface for a time before disappearing back underground, where it gurgled along just below my awareness.

What was it really that sparked my discontent? Was I suddenly dissatisfied with the life of the mind? Or had I caught a glimpse into the academic hall of mirrors that I had unthinkingly allowed to shape my thinking and feeling? Which of my intertwined paths was the selfish and narrow one? For a long time, I was sure that intellectual work was useful only as a form of influence on "real" events. But in the clarity of the backward glance, I can see that world savers and difference makers, especially those who work for large, international institutions, are more highly regarded in our society than high-prestige academics. So I could, for a time, imagine losing a life of books and ideas while gaining points in the social playbook. Of course, I did not see things that way at the time. It was the first of a series of unconscious bargains I struck with myself in the face of profound doubts about my way of living and being.

In the short term, my crisis broke and blemished the smooth surface of my academic accomplishments. When I switched dissertation topics, I lost years of work and had to rush to try to catch up. My ability to speak in public became less reliable and lost its luster, my lack of confidence showing through the cracks. The path to success looked somewhat less automatic; a wrench was in the works. Still, at a moment when the academic job market was relatively stable, not long before the financial collapse that began in 2008, I found a tenure-track job at a large university in the South.

———

After receiving my degree, I found myself in a new town full of strangers, at a university whose overweening passion for football was matched in no other sphere. The streets were wide, the traffic laissez-faire, the sunshine almost constant. Flowering trees and shrubs—dogwood, camellia, and azalea—gave parks and gardens an extravagant beauty, alongside vast stretches of asphalt parking lot, carelessly interspersed with shopping centers. The wound-up impatience I had nurtured in my long years on the East Coast found itself without outlet, and it collided constantly with the local climate of leisured contentment, as stubborn as it was slow.

My job was simpler and less demanding of my time than the work of a graduate student had been. The unfilled hours stretched ahead of me each day, and boredom and loneliness filled the gaps like fog. In a kind of desperate restlessness, I went into the local community as a volunteer—tutoring in a literacy program, visiting the dying in hospices, working at a refugee resettlement center. This person-to-person service was like a slow drip of water on a dry sponge.

A friendship developed between me and a factory worker in her sixties who had an eighth-grade education. She had no use for her studies apart from a love and zeal for the structures of English grammar. She told me that she had sought out tutoring, as I had work as a tutor, out of loneliness and boredom. At the refugee center, the refugees themselves were kept behind thick windows, where they waited for checks or to talk to someone who could untangle their paperwork. I was assigned to organize files for receipts that were duplicated elsewhere—as pointless a task as any I have encountered, and yet I found a peace in it I could not explain.

It was around this time that I rather casually decided that I should have a religion, having grown up without one. I had experimented for a few years with my ancestral religion, Judaism, but lacking either parents or a spouse who practiced, I found no natural entrance to its deepest paths. With some disappointment, I visited some mainline Christian churches, unconsciously moving down an invisible list of major denominations ranked by social status. One church featured a homily on football; another was packed full of visibly wealthy people who showed no sign of spiritual fervor. Both felt like social clubs, a way to feel superior or to feel comfortable. This repelled me, despite—or perhaps because of—my basic interest in social superiority. I wanted something different, something new, without knowing what it was.

One Sunday I attended mass at the local Catholic parish. The church was almost completely silent when I entered and faint sunlight fell on the statues. In the pews around me I saw people of all races and backgrounds—some with families, some alone, many on their knees in quiet prayer. It occurred to me that there was simply no reason for such a random collection of people to be in the same room. We were each of us there alone, and yet united in something invisible and beyond my reach. I decided immediately to begin the process of entering the Catholic Church. I attended the classes for converts at the parish, and in 2006 I was baptized at the long, grand liturgy that Catholics celebrate the night before Easter.

———

At first, I did not connect my interest in having a religion with the existential crisis that I had lived with in some degree for five years. Shortly after my baptism, I moved back to the East, to a new teaching post in Baltimore. I was not there long before the evident poverty and suffering of the city began to unsettle once again my commitment to an academic career track. I visited churches in desolate parts of town, with broken glass in the streets and blocks of boarded-up windows. Unlike the poor neighborhoods deliberately cordoned off—made invisible—in most large American cities, the desolation here stretched on and on, lurking behind every new development. In Baltimore, it was impossible to hide from the sight of poverty or its consequences. The suffering I had imagined previously as exotic, extraordinary, and most of all elsewhere, seemed to have closed in around me.

Under the new aspect of faith, the tensions in me seemed to stretch out to the bounds of the world and to pull at sharp hooks anchored in the depths of my inner life. I began to see that human suffering was not limited to special events and that it could not be ended by reversing particular policies. There was no need to wait for disasters to strike: they were omnipresent, as was responsibility for them. Suffering was a cosmic force, an ever-present reality, Christ crucified at the heart of the world and suffusing it up to the edges. I tried to stop shifting the suffering of others out of view, as had been my constant habit. I began to seek it out, to force myself into regular contact with it.

My frustration with my work, with the focus of my life, thus expanded both in breadth and depth. When I looked to the outside world, I saw tremendous suffering and disorder to which I could make no discernible difference. Nearer by, the shallowness of my academic life became gradually more obvious. Either I sought approval or status by performing well at the expense of others, or in small groups my fellow academics and I explained to one another our own superiority—our difference from the dumb, the wrong, the bad, and the ugly. I remember going to one academic dinner party among many and suddenly feeling queasy as we suggested that the central values in our lives were fine wines and trips to Europe.

I had by this point grown accustomed to being rewarded for my intellectual work with money, status, and privileges. Along the way, my focus had shifted—without my noticing—to the outcomes of my work rather than the work itself. I had lost much of the ability to think freely and openly on a topic, concerned lest I lose my hard-won position in the academic social hierarchy. I worked busily on narrow research projects and did not allow myself the time to read and reflect broadly. My colleagues and I went to exotic destinations as often as possible, seeking out prestigious experiences and high-end consumer goods as a serendipitous perk of participating in an international community of scholars. I visited Lisbon, London, and Berlin; operas, museums, and cabaret shows; and gobbled local delicacies. The tension contracted between these long-established pleasures and my attraction to the hidden world of suffering.

By contrast, as my adventures in volunteering expanded, I met all manner of fascinating strangers who lived outside of middle-class conventions. I got to know a couple at the local Catholic Worker house who had spent decades feeding and serving their neighbors in a particularly desolate neighborhood. Another couple spent their retirement living near a rural prison, hosting families who were visiting the inmates. I volunteered with a four-foot-tall nun, tougher than nails, whose authority dissolved red tape at the women's jail, making possible the movement of ordinary forms of love: clothing, toiletries, conversation, and prayer. I met young men and women who had stepped off prestigious and boring career tracks to live among the poorest people they could find, supported by small donations. Other young people joined them, hungry for alternatives to self-satisfied middle-class life. I encountered by chance a lawyer at the Securities and Exchange Commission who began his workweek by volunteering for the overnight shift at a hospice run by Mother Teresa's nuns. None of these people were much known or recognized—I found them by hard work, punctuated by lucky breaks, rather than through publicity. They worked in hidden corners, invisible to any broader public.

In all these adventures I was still a college professor, lecturing to large classrooms on Plato, Aristotle, and contemporary ethics. The anonymous character of contemporary education for undergraduates clashed sharply with the person-to-person character of my volunteer work and the work of the unusual people that I met. In fact, I think, it was in the classroom, in teaching, that I was in the end ground down the most. In exchange for my comfortable salary, excellent benefits, and ample control over my work schedule, I delivered preprocessed nuggets of knowledge in front of a crowd and doled out above-average grades upon their absorption. The teaching that formed the central activity of my professional life seemed nothing like the lively and collaborative pursuit of ideas that had enchanted me as a student. I still lived the life of the mind, but it tumbled along quietly in the smallish corner of my existence where I worked and collaborated as a scholar. My students saw little of it. As a student myself I had learned habits of mind, a delight in certain passages, a sense of what a good question was, an instinct toward the crucial thing in a book or a poem. I had walked certain ways of reading, thinking, and feeling with my teachers, and had imitated them at close quarters. They knew who I was; I knew who they were; this closeness helped them to communicate appropriate encouragement and discouragement. What were my students learning from me? Not much, I had to conclude, and not often. Not because I didn't care or try, but because the institutional arrangements and baseline expectations made the sort of learning I cared about next to impossible. It was a rare student who chose to break through the culture of anonymity to seek out person-to-person collaboration and guidance.

———

I brought my simmering discontent to the Church's plentiful resources for self-examination and personal growth: prayer and the sacraments, supplemented by retreats, spiritual direction, and Catholic psychotherapy. It took some years to realize that what I had undertaken as a new and curious hobby, practicing a religion, might have the power to recast my troubles with my work and what I felt was the pointlessness of my life.

I learned about the process Catholics call "discerning a vocation," in which through prayer and silence one waits for God to expose one's deepest motivations and so to clarify the shape of one's life. Never short on self-esteem, I was sure that God would want me to do something quite unusual, and that he would not subject me to the same sacrifices as ordinary believers and discerners. I figured I could live in a poor neighborhood as a sort of Catholic anarchist, teaching Greek and Latin out of my living room to the locals. I could marry someone like-minded and raise anarchist children who would help to build a community with the neighbors. When I asked myself where my income would come from, I hit a wall. Who would support such a life? But what else would I do? Remarkable as were the experiments in living I witnessed in my travels, none seemed right for me.

As the years of discontent stretched on, my discomfort grew unbearable. I began to discern religious life, the life of a nun or a sister, trying to face the painful prospect of lifetime celibacy and childlessness. I went first to visit a community of nuns in Switzerland, newly founded in order to promote intellectual life for women in the Church. It was perfect on paper: excellent theology, beautiful liturgies, and an exotic (to me) location. Every day I spent visiting with them I was miserable, for reasons I could not see or understand. The one bright spot was an afternoon when, exploring the town on my own, I found the Western Union where the poor immigrants gathered and did business, and something in me relaxed. I left, uneasy and uncertain, and visited other communities instead. The others lacked the papery perfection of the first and offered no improvement in prospective misery.

After I left the final community on my list, I determined that I should join the community in Switzerland and take my future unhappiness by the horns. When I explained my decision to my spiritual director, he firmly advised against the deliberate choice of a miserable existence. His kind advice made me furious. I slammed the door as I left his office and went to Sunday mass at the church across the street. I knelt in the pew and inwardly raged against my situation. I fumed against the sisters I had met, my felt lack of opportunities, and my apparently unsympathetic spiritual director. My rage burned through the opening hymn and the initial readings. The deacon began to read the Gospel, which turned out to be the Beatitudes, the part of the Sermon on the Mount where Jesus proclaims the blessed happiness of the poor, the weak, the mournful, and the suffering. I suddenly thought of a religious community I had befriended but had scorned as a final destination: Madonna House—poor, humble, unglamorous, and very much lacking in intellectual resources or opportunities. The puzzle pieces of my life fell relentlessly into place. I understood that I could not live a life of the mind and love my neighbors as a hobby. I had had things the wrong way around. I had to love my neighbors and find a mode of intellectual life that expressed that. To do that, I had to put above everything the form of love that goes under the rather cold English name of "charity." I burst into tears.

The moment of discernment went in like an arrow and stuck, and though I was plagued by perfectly justified concerns, nothing could shake me from the decision to go. I took another year, procrastinating anxiously, to put in my last bit of teaching, to squeeze out a last publication, and to take leave from my job. I sold my car, gave away my furniture, put my books in storage, and said goodbye to my friends, I thought, perhaps, for good. On the one hand, once it was all done, I was more relaxed and happier than I had been in years. On the other, a certain terror gripped me: moving into the community felt like casting myself off in the deep water without a life raft.

―――――

During the three years I spent in the Canadian community, a good reader's library and a handful of fascinating conversations were all the intellectual life I had, despite the occasional care package from academic friends, stuffed with issues of the *New Yorker* and photocopied philosophy articles. All that was permitted to me was a full, ordinary human life: work, service, friendship; leisured time in nature; conflict, frustration, and suffering; swimming, crafts, singing in the choir, and radiant, lovingly prepared liturgical celebrations.

In the simplified environment of the community, where no one made money and there was no social ladder to climb, the little human things pushed to the forefront of my awareness. Cleaning or organizing, a walk in the woods, pasting autumn leaves onto cards, even emptying a wastebasket—all became luminous. With an ordered schedule instead of an anxiety-driven slurry of work and entertainment, work could be peaceful and free time spontaneous. With simple necessities provided for, we invented the rest. One true Canadian made a Zamboni from scratch for the ice rink in the marsh, using a pot over a fire for melting snow, a hose, and two perforated pipes with cloth attached to smooth the ice. One of the potters sought paintbrushes with a certain soft texture and so for a time we gathered squirrels that had been killed on the road, for their tails.

It is perhaps a cliché to say that our humanity is displayed best and enjoyed most when faced with serious limitations, but it is true for all that. Without distractions, we notice what is around us. Without rewards, living closely with others, we see how our activities and actions meet or fail to meet real human needs. We become more able to focus on what matters.

To provide for the flourishing of its members and guests, the community had various functioning parts: work, which provided essential goods to ourselves and to our neighbors, but also recreation, games, performances and practical jokes, art and music, prayer and worship. There was to my mind only one human good that was treated more haphazardly in the community than the others: the need to study and learn, in depth, for its own sake.

Deprived of an outlet to use my intellectual training in any social context, I thought hard about the point of higher learning, pondering what connection the professional activities of intellectuals might have with the simple, human reaching out of thought and imagination that I had experienced as a young person. My unusual family notwithstanding, such reaching out is widespread, if not universal. I remembered professional intellectuals, as I was, consumed with the prospect of "making a difference" and so losing touch with what they cared about most. I thought of many academics who fled from the work of the intellect after years of grinding competition and relentless banality.

I remembered other ordinary people—library users, taxi drivers, history buffs, prisoners, stockbrokers—doing intellectual work without recognizing it as such or taking pride in it. I tried to envision what authentic intellectual work might be, how it might draw in ordinary learners without losing its reach to the depths. I pored over my experiences, looking for clues.

One outgrowth of that period of compressed thought was a sudden recognition that I would be happiest teaching at my old liberal arts college, passing on to young people the habits and passions of leisured reflection that I had received myself. So I discerned that it was time to leave the community, and in a nearly miraculous set of coincidences, the job I wanted, along with a house and a car, fell into my lap. The other outgrowth of my experience was the line of thought I explore in this book.

———

Learning is a profession, as I found; it is a way of achieving money and status and of supporting the educational machinery already in place. But it begins in hiding: in the inward thoughts of children and adults, in the quiet life of bookworms, in the secret glances at the morning sky on the way to work, or the casual study of birds from the deck chair. The hidden life of learning is its core, what matters about it. If computers were to collect and organize everything called knowledge—never mind whether it really is knowledge or not—such a collection would be pointless if it did not culminate in someone's personal understanding, if it did not help someone to think about things, to work something out, to reflect. Learning, knowing, studying, and contemplating are activities that live and breathe in individual human beings, even if they are nurtured, cultivated, and preserved in communities and with the help of various instruments. Intellectual activity nurtures an inner life, a human core that is a refuge from suffering as much as it is a resource for reflection for its own sake. There are other ways to nurture the inner life: playing music, or helping the weak and vulnerable, or spending time in nature or prayer—but learning is a crucial one.

When we understand that real learning is hidden learning, that learning at bottom must be withdrawn from the pressure to produce economic, social, or political outcomes, we then face two major difficulties, both practical in nature. First, how exactly is hidden learning achieved or nurtured? How can it be extricated from its technical, professional, and political distortions? It is evident that our human core—our inner resources for thought, reflection, and contemplation—cannot be nurtured by mass education, whether that be online learning or large lecture halls. It must be nurtured person to person or it will largely disappear from ordinary human experience, surviving only in disfigured and marginal ways.

A more fundamental difficulty should be evident from the story of my own struggles as a graduate student. If learning is hidden, what use is it? What good does it do? How does it help mend the suffering fragments of the world? I have perhaps already suggested my answer. If human beings flourish from their inner core rather than in the realm of impact and results, then the inner work of learning is fundamental to human happiness, as far from pointless wheel spinning as are the forms of tenderness we owe our children or grandchildren. Intellectual work is a form of loving service at least as important as cooking, cleaning, or raising children; as essential as the provision of shelter, safety, or health care; as valuable as the delivery of necessary goods and services; as crucial as the administration of justice. All of these other forms of work make possible, but only possible, the fruits of human flourishing in peace and leisure: study and reflection, art and music, prayer and celebration, family and friendship, and the contemplation of the natural world.

Such a vision of the work of the mind leaves it open to anyone who has a desire for it. Intellectual life is not a merely professional activity, to be left to experts. Because its central goods are good universally, it belongs in taxicabs, at the beach house or the book club, in the break room at work, in the backyard of the amateur botanist, in thoughtful reflection whether scattered or disciplined, as much as or more than it does at universities.

The thinking that follows is the outgrowth of my attempts to understand my own intellectual activities and experiences, which have been partly, but not entirely, shaped by faith. The joys of intellectual life were inculcated in me as a child and as a college student with neither roots in nor appeals to revealed religion. In fact, no person in my family in living memory—parent, grandparent, aunt or uncle—practiced such a religion, apart from exactly one Episcopalian great-grandmother who died years before I was born. The principal subjects of my studies and my teaching for many years were the brilliant ancient Greeks, who thought, wrote, lived, and died without any contact with the writings of Jews or Christians. All of that suggests to me that intellectual activity is a natural good, available in general to all human beings. In what follows I have sought out examples, images, stories, and arguments that display the ordinary human character of intellectual goods, leisure, contemplation, and learning. Some of my sources are religious; most are not. It is my hope that all my readers, believer or not, will find these explorations helpful in their own thinking. I can't trace any path that I have not walked myself, but I will leave the doors and windows open.

Introduction

LEARNING, LEISURE, AND HAPPINESS

Some say that a host of horsemen,
others a host of foot-soldiers,
others a host of ships
is the most beautiful thing on the black earth.
But I say it is that thing,
whatever it is,
that one loves.

—SAPPHO, FRAGMENT 16

The Love of Learning

Certain forms of work wear their value on their sleeve. Ironically, these are often those we reward the least: looking after children or the elderly, providing water or electricity, cleaning public bathrooms, collecting garbage, preparing or serving food. Other forms of work may have evident rewards in salary and status, but over the years can leave the stench of pretended usefulness.[1] Which of the forms of work available to us meet or fail to meet real human needs? How do the rewards and visible results of our work connect with their ultimate value? Is there a hidden work that we do, underneath or behind our visible work? How does one become entranced by the rewards of one's work to the point of neglecting its ultimate purpose?

These questions apply to any of us who work, but the work I know is the work of the mind. What does it mean to pursue learning for its own sake? Is it even possible? Is the joy of learning itself selfish? If not, how could the strands of selfishness in it, the rush for achievement, the thrill of competition, be unwound from its heart?

And yet, without visible results, why should intellectual life matter, especially in a world so suffused with suffering? What role could it or should it play in repairing the broken fragments of our communities or in pushing back the darkness at their margins? These questions, along with a host of others that arise from them, shape the chapters that follow.

———

What does learning look like, stripped of its trappings of fame, prestige, fortune, and social use? In other words, how is it good for its own sake, because of its effect on the learner rather than because of its outward results?

I say "its effect on the learner," but that phrase of course raises further questions. What sort of effect are we looking for? If learning is simply a pleasure, like a foot massage or a walk on the beach, would that suffice to account for its value? I think not, because a human being must be more than a vehicle of its own pleasure. Questions about what is valuable in itself for human beings have to do with *what a human being is* and what *our* ultimate value is. These are huge questions, to the point of being indigestible. They have to be nibbled around rather than gulped all at once. For now, it will be enough to try to isolate what is called the intrinsic value of learning, its value apart from the visible or outward results.

We all know examples of learning loved for itself. We see the love of learning in children collecting and cataloging dead bugs, or in bookworms as they huddle in closets and corners, hiding from their public lives as shop owners, politicians, or housewives. A bird watcher with his binoculars and guidebook lives a life of learning, as does a hobbyist modeling historically accurate toy soldiers, carefully researching period costumes and hairstyles. So too does an artist who ponders the shape of a tree in order to capture its color and movement, or a novelist who soaks herself in an urban community in order to untangle and dramatize its elements. Hippies hunger to learn when they travel the world in search of the meaning of life. Distracted mathematicians exercise the love of learning as they manipulate strange symbols and disclose what lies under the surface of things; so does the philosophical teenager who suddenly wonders what numbers are.

I've mentioned characteristic forms of learning for its own sake: mathematical proofs or calculations; the study of the natural world; thoughtful reflection on experience; reading books, or, at least, reading good books. These activities are aimed at certain objects: mathematical objects, principles, and proofs; the behavior of animals, plants, and materials; and the ruminations on human life found in works of literature, philosophy, or history. But we desire to learn for as many reasons as there are things to desire. Consider the overzealous explainer, always anxious to correct us, saying "Actually, . . ." We suspect that he uses learning as a form of social domination, perhaps to compensate for status lost in athletic or erotic contests. More generally, a spy reads a work of literature to get inside the mind-set of her target; a quant on Wall Street fiercely calculates risks to maximize profits; a political activist pores over scientific literature seeking evidence that supports his cause; a mafia boss studies the chemistry of decomposition to get rid of a body. These are not exercises of the love of learning but are undertaken for different goals: military victory, wealth, political success, escaping the notice of the law. So we call such uses of the intellect *instrumental*; they are motivated by results and outcomes, whatever the intensity of their pursuit. By contrast, the hidden life of learning involves some savoring of its natural objects—people, numbers, God, nature—for their own sake.

A person can do mathematics without doing it thoughtfully and reflectively, caught instead in a fear- and shame-driven race for achievement. Such is the life of learning offered by much or most of our educational system. On its own, it is not learning for its own sake any more than is the activity of spies, Wall Street quants, or political activists. On the other hand, a person can start out on a project as a mere means to an end and find herself appreciating the activity for itself. The outcome-driven math student can catch on to the beauty of math, the pleasure of proof and calculation, and so open up the inner activity of learning sought for its own sake. So too the teenager longing for the love and approval of his peers can read a book just to impress someone and find himself caught by something deeper. Consider comedian Steve Martin's description of how he became a philosophy major thanks to the influence of his girlfriend, Stormie:

> If Stormie had said I would look good in a burgundy ball gown, I would have gone out and bought a burgundy ball gown. Instead, she suggested I read W. Somerset Maugham's *The Razor's Edge*. *The Razor's Edge* is a book about a quest for knowledge. Universal, final, unquestionable knowledge. I was swept up in the book's glorification of learning and the idea that, like a stage magician, I could have secrets possessed only by a few.[2]

Martin starts out trying to please his girlfriend and ends up discovering a passion for learning that shapes his young life. But his interest in philosophy outlasts the relationship that inspired it; it would be a mistake to see it as inauthentic, as a mere attempt to please someone else, because of the way it was discovered.

Jack London tells a similar story in his semiautobiographical novel *Martin Eden*. The working-class protagonist is invited to a wealthy stranger's house, where he examines a pile of alluring books and meets a beautiful young woman. He falls in love with both and undertakes a grueling self-directed course of reading for her sake. But as it turns out, the books unlock a highly critical and brilliant individual with whom the wealthy young woman is incompatible. Eden's development exposes a rift between the carefully policed gentility of the educated middle classes and the wild and open possibilities of intellectual development. His progress into a suicidal disillusionment also points to a danger of a life of learning: an alienation that breeds arrogance and contempt for others.

Save the dangers for later: for now, it is enough to notice from these two stories that we form ourselves—our talents, our interests, and our characteristic activities—from humble, nakedly instrumental beginnings: from getting what we want, avoiding humiliation, and seeking love, approval, and social advancement. They open up doorways in us, desires, concerns, sources of wonder that we did not know were there. Activities catch on in this way because they meet a natural need in us. Our natural needs often lie buried; something from the outside attracts us, or shatters or breaks through the obstacles, so that those needs are brought to the surface. Steve Martin's passion is to think philosophically about the world, while Martin Eden's is to capture life in words; neither could be described as primarily concerned with the instrumental uses of learning. Both are changed and reoriented by what they discover in themselves.

Something in us, then, wants to learn for its own sake, even if we embark on that learning for the sake of some smaller end.

But the possibility of using mathematics or science or literature for the sake of money, grades, love, or murder means that the subjects alone don't define what intellectual life is. It is crucial that reading or calculating or learning be undertaken in a thoughtful or a contemplative spirit. Nor indeed is it necessary to focus on these typical objects. A person can learn, and relish his learning, while engaging in any activity whatsoever. Should we think of the guiding motivation, the thoughtful spirit, as more important than a typical set of objects? Perhaps we could say that the love of learning can be exercised in any activity—one's daily work, watching sports, taking out the trash, reading potboilers— so long as it is approached reflectively or thoughtfully, so long as one relishes learning from it.

This second approach also faces difficulties. Is it an exercise of the love of learning to go on a week-long drunken bender as a part of a journey of self-understanding? Can one play video games in a contemplative spirit? The answer, of course, is yes— but the activities are not quite fitting to their contemplative goal. The mismatch is shown by the kind of pressure they exert on the prospective inquirer, a pressure opposite to that felt by our status-driven math student. Mathematics draws the competitive student into appreciating it for its own sake. By contrast, our inquirer undertakes video games to understand better their appeal to human nature, but finds herself drawn into the compulsive pursuit of distraction, to cascading, increasingly joyless victories in pixels. Likewise, it would take an unusual discipline to maintain contemplative distance from one's own drunken bender. The FBI agent investigating illegal pornography looks at the images differently than an avid consumer would. But it is evident that the force of those images, despite the agent's investigatory commitment, makes the work difficult.

We tend to think of the objects of our desires as items in a restaurant buffet—perhaps some of this, perhaps some of that. But our desires and their objects are more like rivers. They have a force and pressure all their own. Once we set out on them, they pull us along in a particular direction, opening up possibilities to us that we did not expect or choose. This simple psychological fact is the reason why there is such a thing as education—why using our minds, or learning to paint, or losing weight requires not only discipline and social incentives but also the guidance of wise elders who know what lies along certain pathways, and who are willing to expose their own ignorance and uncertainty when guiding the young.

Ends, Means, and Ultimate Goals

How ought we describe this human need, the appetite for learning and understanding, in a way that illuminates its typical forms and deviations? I follow a tradition originating with Plato and Aristotle that distinguishes types of desire by their *final end*.[3] We do many things instrumentally, for the sake of something else: eat breakfast to calm hunger pains, exercise to stay healthy, work for money, have children to placate a spouse or fit in with the Joneses. Other things we do for their own sake: play cards, or go for hikes; read, or build model airplanes. Some things evidently are both instrumental and for their own sake: we have children also for their own sake; we work for money, but sometimes also for the love of our work activities themselves; we fish to eat, but also for the sport of it.

Our actions and activities are affected by our goal in pursuing them. There is a difference in character between a targeted trip to the grocery store to get a bottle of milk and a more contemplative shopping trip in which one explores unusual products on the shelves and talks to neighbors in the aisles. A hiking expedition with friends differs from one with an important business client. A marriage of convenience differs from a marriage for love. Thus each action or activity has an end goal that gives it a certain character.

To some extent, we choose the goals we pursue and how to pursue them. But there are natural tensions and natural affinities between certain goals and certain means of pursuit. Hence the discomfort of the marriage of convenience, the difficulty of enjoying a long commute by car for its own sake; or, by contrast, the ease of pausing to enjoy a beautiful landscape, the naturalness of putting a child's good ahead of one's own. Plato and Aristotle and many after them sought something they called the highest good—the best human activity, pursued for its own sake—for which we have a natural affinity above all others. Such a good would be something in which one's whole life would culminate, a form of secure happiness built into who we are and what we want.

Why would we think we have a highest good or an ultimate end at which our activities aim? We have many end goals, often at the same time, but certain goals have a structuring or ordering effect on others. We choose our career to permit leisure time with our family, or we choose a less demanding family to allow free upward growth in our careers. Our ultimate end—family in the first case, success in the second—frames and structures our other pursuits. We trade a freer schedule for more money, or sacrifice a higher salary for more time to pursue our heart's desire. The structuring effect of some goals over others suggests that we have a *basic orientation* that is determined by our ultimate end, the goal (assuming there is one) that structures all of our other choices. Such a goal is our highest good, whether we have chosen it as such or it has grown higgledy-piggledy out of personal or social pressures. That highest good or ultimate end might be wealth, status, or family life; serving our community or the enjoyment of the natural world; knowledge of God, or pleasure and partying, or writing novels, or the pursuit of mathematical truth. Like any smaller end, our ultimate end might be better or worse suited to satisfy us.

If we do not believe that we have a single basic orientation, it is very difficult to understand common stories about how our lives change. We turn from a life of crime to a life of penance. We quit drinking and become a faithful neighborhood volunteer. We have children and we abandon pursuits we once found all-absorbing, perhaps working less, perhaps withdrawing from our hard-partying friends; perhaps we draw closer to family members or put down roots in our community. Orientations do not, of course, always change for the better. Sometimes we take a turn fundamentally for the worse. Disillusionment with love or with work can drive us to drink, or to work compulsively, or to seek one restless thrill after another. The political worker begins in the hope of building a just society on earth, and ends up a functionary or an apparatchik.

The change in orientation need not be dramatic; our values can slowly corrode in the wrong environment, or a seed of joy can take root under our radar, blossoming unexpectedly years later. Some life changes may be only superficially dramatic. Certain status seekers find their way to the top no matter what the outward value structure of their institution: they succeed in the fascist dictatorship and the new democracy, the traditional church and the church in reform. But conversions, reversions, corruption, and disillusionment are widespread phenomena. It is hard to believe that they are not real possibilities for all of us, and hard to make sense of those possibilities if we do not have a basic orientation to begin with.

We may resist the idea that we have a single ultimate end. Surely, we think, although some goals structure others, we can have more than one that matters most to us. We prize family *and* work above all, or philosophy *and* social justice. No single end dominates. At best, such a life will be rare if it is not impossible. There is a fact about how our lives are ordered: not what we want our final end to be, nor what we think it is, but which end is at bottom structuring the other ends. Even if we feel that we have achieved a rare and fine balance, there is a fact about what we would choose if our most basic priorities came into conflict. It is a matter of what we are disciplined or not disciplined to choose, a matter of an embodied excellence or a lack of one. We see our ultimate end only when wishful thinking dissolves in the face of a real choice.

I can of course make mistakes about which activities are compatible with my ultimate end. I may choose to have children thinking that I will be able to maintain the inner space to pursue my mathematical interest, and I might be wrong. Since children generate moral duties, I may not be able to recover my original mathematical focus without wronging my children. Likewise, I may choose not to have children with the thought that I will be better able to write poetry without distraction, but I may find that in domestic isolation my life experience becomes narrow, shallow, and impoverished, and my well of creativity dries up. Our ultimate ends are often fragile in unpredictable ways; hence our youthful anxiety about the future, our midlife crises, and our regrets in old age.

We may not have any idea of what our basic orientation consists in, or what ultimate end may be structuring our life unbeknownst to us. Our motives are always mixed and our ultimate goals are often obscure. Often we cannot admit to ourselves that, say, status, or money, or drinking matters most to us. But even apart from conversions or breakdowns, certain conflicts or crises suggest that we have such an end and what it is. My choice of one thing over another reveals yet more ultimate goals. Say I skip my child's piano recital for an afternoon at the bar, or to finish a work project that feels necessary. Or the business client cancels our hike—do I go on the hike anyway? If I don't, perhaps I was less interested in nature than in the deal I was planning to cut. I choose a high-status job and do it with a commitment to high moral principle. I discover immoral behavior there whose exposure will lose me everything. Do I keep my morals, or the job and the status?

Our ultimate end can be displayed by our choices as the thing to which we are most fundamentally committed, something for which, when the chips are down, we will sacrifice anything else. It may be only at points of conflict or times of trial where we discover what in the soup of our conflicting desires and pursuits matters most to us. We promise "till death do us part" when our love is young and good-looking and when life is full of promise, but it is in failure or decrepitude or at the hospital bed that we learn what we meant and why.

Leisure

In our pursuit of the basic forms and deviations of intellectual life, we have distinguished instrumental pursuits—things we do as means to ends—from ends, or pursuits worthy in themselves. We have also begun to look at ways in which a particular pursuit can shape and structure a life, so that some activity is our ultimate end and shapes our basic orientation. What would happen if we tried to organize our lives around merely instrumental pursuits, such as earning money or promoting justice? Aristotle argued that our ultimate end had to be sought for its own sake, or our actions would turn out to be empty and vain. It's clear enough that my actions are vain when I don't achieve my small-scale goal. If I pack my swim bag, put on shoes, get my keys, and drive my car to the pool only to find it closed, my end goal of swimming is frustrated, and my string of actions is in vain. Likewise, if my ultimate goal is not sought for its own sake, it seems that many or most of my actions are in vain. Suppose the pool is open and I get to swim: Why do I do it? I swim for the sake of health. I want to be healthy so I can work. I work for the sake of money. And the money is for the sake of the food, drink, housing, recreation, and exercise—all of which make it possible for me to work.

I have described a life of utter futility. If I work for the sake of money, spend money on basic necessities for life, and organize my life around working, then my life is a pointless spiral of work for the sake of work. It is like buying ice cream, immediately selling it for cash, and then spending the proceeds on ice cream (which one once again sells, . . . and so on). It is no less tragic than working for money and getting crushed by a falling anvil on the way to cash the paycheck. Activities are not worthwhile unless they culminate in something satisfying. For that reason, Aristotle argued that there must be something beyond work—the use of leisure, for the sake of which we work and without which our work is in vain. Leisure is not merely recreation, which we might undertake for the sake of work—to relax or rest before beginning to labor anew. Rather, leisure is an inward space whose use could count as the culmination of all our endeavors. For Aristotle, only contemplation—the activity of seeing and understanding and savoring the world as it is—could be the ultimately satisfying use of leisure.

Despite a long tradition of thinking that Aristotle helped to inspire, the kind of leisure that functions as an ultimate goal of

living does not require vast estates and the life of a country gentleman. It can be taken in a moment, or in a long pause; it can
fruitfully coexist with certain kinds of manual labor. The great
books movement that for a time shaped American intellectual
culture began among working people, in workmen's institutes
where people who toiled with their hands sought to develop
themselves as human beings with rich inner lives.[4]

In his classic handbook for amateur intellectuals, *The Intellectual Life*, the Dominican priest A. G. Sertillanges claimed that
an intellectual vocation could be lived on two hours of free time
a day—and so is compatible with both work and family life.[5] His
secular contemporary, Arnold Bennett, claimed in *How to Live
on 24 Hours a Day* that it would suffice to take a daily half hour
of focused thinking, combined with three evening sessions a
week during which one read seriously for ninety minutes.[6] I think
that Bennett and Sertillanges are right—and even beyond what
they imagined, one can aim at leisure and use it fruitfully without the full undertaking of an intellectual vocation. Leisure can
be savored in a moment, or in a long pause, or in a restful chew-
ing over of the events of the day. A weekend in the woods can
allow the insight that was gathering, hidden in our daily busyness,
to blossom. Despite ancient prejudice against it, manual labor
leaves the mind free to ruminate and consider in a way that other
forms of labor do not. This is why carpentry, or gardening, or
housecleaning can be satisfying in a way that ticking boxes,
pushing paper, or thinking through complex but trivial problems
is not.

That said, under certain circumstances leisure does not exist,
and so its use is impossible. Pursuing the necessities of life can
be utterly overwhelming. This is particularly true if one has to
work at an exploitative job. In *Martin Eden*, Jack London describes his protagonist Martin studying fervently to educate

himself, both for his own sake and to make him worthy of the woman he loves. Gradually he runs out of money. He takes up a job in a laundry that requires fourteen hours of solid, concentrated work six days a week. Having previously lived on only five hours of sleep, he is confident upon taking the job that he can continue to read after work. After one day in the laundry, the powers of concentration necessary for him to read evaporate. After one week, he no longer has the energy even to think: "There was no room in his brain for the universe and its mighty problems. All the broad and spacious corridors of his soul were closed and hermetically sealed."[7] After three weeks of this routine, Martin returns to drinking after a long abstinence, and he finds in drunkenness the imagination, warmth, wonder, and beauty that the laundry work has driven out of him.

London's account is fictional or semifictional, but it closely matches the real-life experiences of others. For example, George Orwell writes of his stint in the kitchen of a Paris hotel, where employees at his level work eighty to one hundred hours a week, leaving no time to think, and no money to save up for a family or for a change of career. Their lives are wasted in exhausting work from which drink and sleep are the only refuge.[8] Barbara Ehrenreich describes her experience at the end of two shifts of waitressing: "I am not tired at all, I assure myself, though it may be that there is simply no more 'I' left to do the tiredness monitoring."[9] Or consider the journalist James Bloodworth's recent account of working as a "picker" in an Amazon warehouse.[10] After days of walking or running for many miles over long hours, under constant electronic surveillance, penalized for bathroom breaks and illness, and on a schedule made unpredictable by the prospects of canceled shifts or compulsory overtime, Bloodworth finds himself mentally and physically exhausted. Quick thrills that he and his coworkers might have otherwise limited or shunned become extremely attractive. As one of his coworkers put it, "This work makes you want to drink."[11]

Leisure can be destroyed in appalling working conditions designed by others. Leisure can also be destroyed by anxieties imposed, through no fault of our own, in the crush of life. It can be destroyed by compulsive behaviors that consume all of our thought and awareness. Leisure can also be destroyed by our own choices. Aristotle's teacher Plato, through the mouth of Socrates, describes philosophical leisure by contrast to the experience of someone immersed in lawcourts and in various forms of social striving. To a philosopher, a leisured person, it does not matter:

> whether they talk for a day or for a year, if only they may hit on that which is. But the other—the man of the law courts— is always in a hurry when he is talking; he has to speak with one eye on the clock. Besides, he can't make speeches on any subject he likes; he has his adversary standing over him, armed with compulsory powers and with the sworn statement, which is read out point by point as he proceeds, and must be kept to by the speaker.[12]

The unleisurely life of the lawcourts, hurried and constrained by the demands of others, is evidently the product of education and choice, not of externally imposed economic circumstances.

We have contemporary parallels to the voluntary slavery of Plato's lawcourts. Consider the world of urban tech workers described in Lauren Smiley's 2015 essay "The Shut-In Economy."[13] Many such workers work from home and live by themselves. To save time, they use numerous apps for everyday tasks such as ordering meals, grocery shopping, and simple household organization. Today's Martin Edens, the low-paid delivery workers, drivers, and cleaners, must stack job upon job just to meet the cost of necessities. But those they serve, the urban tech workers, do not save time for the purpose of leisured contemplation or wholesome hobbies, but rather in order to work even more. Smiley describes one tech worker who has determined that for every hour that she saves by outsourcing her personal and household tasks, she can make $1000 for her company. So she works eleven-hour days and uses app services to run her errands, do her hair, and straighten her home.

The "masters" of our current servant class have no leisure either. The slave is a slave of a slave, and these days at the top of heap of the slaves there is not even an exploitative gentleman farmer—writing essays, dissecting animals, and speculating on the nature of the political—but another slave at a higher social rank. The wealthier in the chain impose such burdens on themselves, just as many of us in positions of privilege willingly put ourselves under electronic surveillance as constant as the Amazon warehouse, posting to social media even our time at the gym or our obsessions with our pets.[14]

By contrast, the office job that was more common in previous decades may be deadly boring in itself, but it leaves clear an inward space for other routes of development. John Baker worked for many years pushing paper at the Automobile Association in Essex, and in his spare time looked at birds with systematic personal and contemplative intensity. He followed peregrine falcons by bicycle, carrying maps, eyeglasses, and voluminous notebooks. The result was the extraordinary poetic reflection published in his 1967 book, *The Peregrine*. The poets Wallace Stevens (an insurance agent) and Frank O'Hara (an art curator) squeezed their poetry into the spare moments permitted by ordinary, busy working life. Stevens claimed he wrote poems "just about anywhere," and got his poetic ideas on walks. Nor, for Stevens at least, was the squeezing of poetry to the margins of his time a compromise. He told a journalist a few years before his death, "It gives a man character as a poet to have this daily contact with a job."[15] His fellow poet John Ashbery described Frank O'Hara as "dashing the poems off at odd moments—in his office at the Museum of Modern Art, in the street at lunchtime or even in a room full of people—he would then put them away in drawers and cartons and half forget them."[16] O'Hara's capacity for poetry seems to have been built into his life; he found pauses, moments of leisure, that were invisible to others.

The patron saint of overworked teachers, Alice Kober, taught five classes at a time at Brooklyn College in the 1940s.[17] At any rate, she taught during the day. At night, she set about deciphering an ancient language, Linear B, that had been uncovered on clay tablets at the turn of the century and that stood as a Mount Everest for linguists, a seemingly impossible puzzle. A middle-aged spinster, the daughter of working-class immigrants, she collected the statistics for each sign of the dead language onto two hundred thousand paper slips. Because of paper shortages during and after the war these slips had to be repurposed from any spare paper she could find. The slips in turn were collected into old cigarette cartons. Her work was cut off by an untimely illness, but she laid the foundation for the dramatic decipherment that took place only a few years after her death.

Sometimes leisure appears as a disciplined, nearly impossible achievement. The twelfth-century Holy Roman emperor Frederick the Second took time out from amassing vast territory and influence to have a long discussion with Leonardo of Pisa, the mathematician known as Fibonacci, and he himself made long ornithological studies for a still-unrivaled treatise on falconry.[18] Indeed, leisure can emerge for contemplation even in the worst circumstances imaginable. The psychologist Victor Frankl wrote of what he called "the intensification of inner life" as a prisoner in Auschwitz. He meant in part his feelings for loved ones and remembered images of a life with dignity. He describes how vivid the beauty of trees and sunsets became to the prisoners, of the choices prisoners had to make to resist the overwhelming dehumanizing character of their surroundings.[19]

The robustness of the capacity of human beings to savor, contemplate, and enjoy indicates its natural depth in us. Like the right kind of hiking and the authentic love of learning, leisure can in principle be found and used anywhere, but it thrives only under certain conditions: free time, exposure to the outdoors, and a certain mental emptiness.

Leisure, Recreation, and Happiness

The leisure activities that count as a culminating end of life have a sort of timelessness. When we are at leisure, we stop counting the minutes toward the goal, because the goal is precisely what we are doing: hiking in the wilderness, engaging in thoughtful conversation with oneself or with others, sitting around the fire with those we love. Sometimes, leisure takes the form of an intense activity. Staying up all night talking, cataloging the weeds in the garden, John Baker's bird-watching—all may be undertaken with great energy. The freedom of a leisurely activity is the freedom from results or outcomes beyond it, not the freedom of rest or recreation.

Recreation, too, has its timelessness. There is no obvious point at which one has completed a beach holiday, where time stretches out in waves, sand, and sunshine. Time drops away in a night of fierce card playing, as it does at the afternoon cookout. What is the difference between a relaxing activity and the form of leisure that constitutes the end of one's life? The difference is simply that we would not judge a cookout or the beach holiday or card playing to be the pinnacle of life. These activities are lovely, human, and necessary, but they do not draw on our highest capacities. Art, music, serious conversation, and loving service, by contrast, bring out the best in us. They are goals toward which we strive; they are engines for limitless personal growth. The difference between leisure and recreation will be subtle, but clear, in how we choose these different kinds of ends. Any minimally happy life must include recreation, but what really matters is far more demanding.

It is the highest goods that may require us to turn our lives upside down, to sacrifice not only time and money but friends, loved ones, social stature, and sometimes our own lives. Khaled Al-Asaad, director of antiquities at the ancient site of Palmyra in Syria for many years, was captured by members of ISIS and tortured in an attempt to make him reveal the locations of valuable artifacts. He refused, and was murdered. Al-Asaad died, it seems, for history, for knowledge, and for art.[20] By contrast, it is not in general reasonable to die for a good game of cards or for a birthday party at the beach. That said, one could imagine conditions so oppressive that the little human things are the only humanity one has, and so are worth dying for. In those cases, one dies not for the birthday party or the card game as such but for the full scope of humanity that they suggest, the dignity denied by one's circumstances.

Aristotle thought that our ultimate end constituted our conception of happiness. That is, we hold as our ultimate end whatever we believe a happy life to consist in. He also believed that human nature gave happiness definite contours: some ultimate ends will be satisfying, and others not. Our conception of happiness can be wrong. Contemplation, in his view, was the only thing that could structure other human desires so that a human life would be satisfying. All the same, if our nature is divided, as he thought it was (and as it obviously is), if our motives are various and conflicting, and if our desires generate perceptions of reality and perceptions of value, real happiness will be very difficult both to discern and to achieve.

It is true that Aristotle conceived of contemplation too narrowly: sophisticated philosophy of the kind he practiced himself forms the core of his notion of happiness. But it is evident that contemplation can be the relishing of the beauty of one's family and its common life; the sophisticated calculations of the physicist; the admiration of the curve of the wood being shaped into furniture; the nun singing the Psalms five times a day; the therapist or teacher poring over their human examples.

Even so, it may seem too much to accept that contemplation is the one true good for human beings. It has been hard, after all, for many to accept; it is a countercultural and counterintuitive proposal, both now and at most times in the past. But while the proposal lies in the background of this book and haunts it, so to speak, you, my reader, need not accept it. You may think that happiness must consist in more than one good. You may judge that happiness is universally desirable, but that not everyone has a taste for learning in itself. Or you may think that "happiness" itself is a fantasy that we only torture ourselves trying to attain. But I do think it ought to be clear by the end of this book that contemplation in the form of learning is a robust human good, valuable for its own sake and worthy of time and resources. Its degree of centrality in a given human life I leave up in the air. I try to leave it so, at any rate. Sometimes my own enthusiasms will draw my thumb to the scale.

The Specter of Elitism

The praise of learning for its own sake as necessary for a flourishing life is often charged with displaying an aristocratic bias, as if aristocratic Aristotle's endorsement was the kiss of moral death, as if a truth could not be tangled up with moral ugliness. But the accounts I alluded to of the destruction of leisure in the lives of modern workers, the diminishment of their humanity, ought to make us more alive to the value of leisure, not less. Hearing such stories, we ought to be motivated to promote sufficient time for all workers to think, to savor, to reflect, to pursue wholesome pastimes—not simply a lucky and special few. The philosopher Simone Weil, reflecting on a failed attempt to educate workers, wrote:

> Is this a reason to condemn all work of this kind? On the contrary, the important thing is to distinguish, among the attempts at working-class culture, those that are conducted in such a way as to strengthen the ascendancy of the intellectuals over the workers, and those conducted in such a way as to free the workers from this domination.[21]

Weil makes a distinction that modern educators who seek to provide professional training for the disadvantaged would do well to keep this in mind. Do we seek to elevate those among the poor who are worthy of dominating others? Or do we seek to diminish the difference between the social classes altogether?

The idea that real and serious learning is something practiced only by a small elite is stubborn and hard to displace. But it is false. Consider Mendel Nun, a fisherman on a kibbutz in the Galilee, born just after the First World War. He found ancient stone anchors as he fished and collected them into what is now a small museum. Seeking to understand what he found, he studied the sources on fishing in antiquity and, since this was a rare interest, he became one of its foremost experts.[22] I imagine that this intellectual project, discovered in the course of his daily work, changed how he lived. A simple fishing outing would be seen in its breadth and depth, as a human enterprise grown out of its thousand-year past and built into his surroundings.

In my home country, the United States, perfectly ordinary people pack up their telescopes in summertime and head for star parties in dark rural areas, seeking out supernovas, double stars, and unusual planetary conjunctions. Travel to Gettysburg and you will find thousands upon thousands of supposed normals who suddenly want to know everything about a battle that took place 150 years ago: the human fighters and the human dead, their clothes, their weapons, their stratagems, victories, and failures. I spent a summer in Israel, and there it is archaeology that holds the popular imagination: crowds tolerate unbearable heat to hear this stone or that stone, this hill or that valley, tell stories that books alone don't tell. The charge that religion is anti-intellectual is widespread and ancient, and yet I've met few ordinary believers who weren't curious about why there are two creation stories in Genesis, or what kind of thing a "satan" is, or what the shewbreads in the Temple of Jerusalem were for.

Behind the sea of details in the pursuit of astronomy, history, archaeology, and religion lie fundamental questions: Where did the universe come from? Are the vast galaxies the product of chance or design? What makes war, the greatest of human evils, possible? What could make it seem morally necessary? In Israel, I asked an archaeologist what drove her to sift through dirt in hundred-degree heat and spend countless hours classifying shards of pottery. She told me: "I'm interested in ancient economy. What I want to understand is this: Money makes people and their communities great. But it also is the source of evil and destruction. How is it possible? How do good and evil mix in a human being?"

The love of learning is general among human beings and pursued in a variety of ways and degrees. Unlike the love of the outdoors, however, we do not always recognize it. We miss it in its lowlier forms, and misidentify it in its higher ones. We do so because we have various desires and goals, in various invisible hierarchies. We have ultimate ends that may or may not be transparent to us. Thus we can love learning for its own sake, or we can use it for the sake of a political agenda; it can be a means to wealth and status, or a stepping-stone to a sense of achievement; learning can accrue under idle social habits, following the crowds. We may not know whether we are driven by the real thing or by something else until we are put to the test. But to limit learning to the professionals would be like considering sponsored mountain climbers to be the only true appreciators of the outdoors.

This philosophical introduction to the intrinsic value of learning and its nearby companions leisure and contemplation is meant to help the reader navigate the examples of learning for its own sake that follow. What does an authentic exercise of the love of learning look like in real life? How might that exercise shape a person's life? How might the love of learning, well exercised, itself be a tonic to alleviate futile ways of life or unavoidable forms of suffering? How could its exercise count as the culmination of a person's entire endeavor?

But the examples that I present will only raise more questions. How does it happen that the love of learning gets corrupted by the pursuit of wealth or power? Does intellectual activity lie in a natural tension with ordinary human communities? In the second chapter of this book, I attempt a diagnosis of the corruption of learning by the love of money and status. I then tell two stories of the conversion or redemption of intellectual life, one through the famous story of Saint Augustine, the other through the modern secular account of the origins of the work of art in Ferrante's Neapolitan novels.

Last, I will turn to a third set of questions. What haunts modern people with intellectual inclinations most is the sense that the pursuit of learning for its own sake is useless and thus unjustified in the face of the enormous demands that human suffering and injustice place on us. I distinguish a superficial sense of "making a difference" from forms of person-to-person service, suggesting that intellectual life is useful when it sees itself and orders itself as the latter.

Professional academics are the natural stewards of the activities focused on books and ideas. And many academics these days find themselves discouraged and restless as I was. I am convinced that the ailment is largely a matter of affect and with it a failure of imagination. Our marriage to intellectual work has grown stale and lifeless. Our eyes wander restlessly to other prospects. We wonder whether we missed a turn somewhere. Surely farming would be more fulfilling, or singing in a nightclub; surely our talents would be better used in the vast global machinery of human rights work. Under the circumstances, a brilliant philosophical argument—even if I could make one—would be useless. Likewise, a thorough historical diagnosis—an account of the twists and turns of cultural and economic life that brought us to our sad pass—might make us wiser, but it will not restore our lost spark. It is images and models that we need: attractive fantasies to set us in a certain direction and to draw us on, reminders of who we once were and who or what we might be. Only then will the romance return.

Learning and intellectual life are not the exclusive province of professional academics, but academics are their official guardians; and so a good place to begin renewal from. But I hope also that this book will fall into the hands of nonprofessionals with intellectual interests, and that they will recognize themselves in it. Perhaps we will be even better off if intellectual life is renewed from the grassroots.

My concern for images and stories in what follows is indifferent regarding whether they are historical or fictional. That is in part because I have become unsure as to the essential difference between them. Good fiction resonates in truth; good history tells affecting stories. So, too, literary images inspire real-life models, and vice versa. Our lives are responsive to books; books in turn reflect our lives.

I will leave my life story behind in the book that follows. A wider cast of characters will accompany you, as they have me, on my inquiry into what intellectual life is and what role it plays in a happy human life and in a flourishing human community.

I choose the word "inquiry" carefully, since it is my hope that you, my reader, will inquire with me. After all, each person lives his or her own life, especially in the use of the mind. I may find myself at an impasse where you see a way through. Where I find clarity, you may find an obstacle. Many of my thoughts will be only half-baked. Their batter may not be even quite mixed. Finish baking them your own way—or cook up something else.

CHAPTER 1

A Refuge from the World

Now the members of this small group have tasted how sweet and blessed a possession philosophy is, and at the same time they have also seen the madness of the multitude and realized, in a word, that no one does anything sane, sound, or right in public affairs and that there is no ally with whom they might go to the aid of justice and survive. Instead they'd perish before they could profit either their city or their friends, and be useless both to themselves and others, just like a man who has fallen among wild animals and is neither willing to join them in doing injustice nor sufficiently strong to oppose the general savagery alone.

For all these reasons I say the philosopher remains quiet and minds his own affairs. Like someone who takes refuge under a little wall from a storm of dust or hail driven by the wind, seeing others filled with lawlessness, he is satisfied if he can somehow lead his present life free from injustice and impious acts and depart from it with good hope, blameless and content.

—PLATO, *REPUBLIC* 6, 496D

The World

In a luxury apartment building in Paris, the residents—civil servants, lawyers, aristocrats—prepare for a day of meetings. An hour spent with the newspapers is the prologue to conversations with lobbyists, legislators, board members, clients, partners in enterprise. Chips move on the game board. Victories turn to losses, losses to victories. The game plan on which everything was staked shifts; another game plan is adopted. Buzzwords are replaced by slogans, slogans by buzzwords. Someone makes money, someone loses money, someone wins a vote, another loses his seat. The men of consequence (they are, generally, men) return home to wives riddled with neuroses, seeking one salve for anxiety after another: special diets, yoga, psychotherapy, medication, jogging, adultery, mindfulness. Their children too are anxious, working around the clock for the approval of their teachers, hoping to advance with honors to the next stage. Their futures stretch before them as an indefinite series of prizes to be won or lost, with infinite and infinitely fascinating gradations of value in between. In the early mornings come invisible cleaning ladies to scrub toilets and do laundry, plumbers to service the pipes, electricians to maintain the wires. The locksmith oils a door and changes a lock. Nameless drivers pull up and pull away. The concierge of the building takes notes from the residents, calls the workmen, instructs the cleaning lady, collects the mail.

Ancient Athens has been made rich by the spoils of empire. The men who beat back the Persian invaders, invented scientific speculation, and wrote magnificent tragedies are now dead or nearly so. Their wealthy sons waste away their time in chariot racing and horsemanship, or they learn the arts of speaking in order to squeeze out a greater share of the winnings of war. The community that once shared its burdens and distributed its spoils has divided into bands of rich and poor, each looking sharply to the disadvantage of the other, each awaiting its chance.

In Roman Palestine, a very young woman, having reached the age of fertility, prepares for marriage. She will be transferred from the service of her parents to that of her husband, expected to bear him sons until she dies. Perhaps then her husband will take another wife. When her sons are grown, they too will find wives to provide them sons, and so on and so on, ad infinitum.

In central Europe at the turn of the twentieth century, scientific discovery is at an apex. The cell and the bacterium have become visible, along with the cures for numerous diseases and infirmities. Electric and magnetic forces have been captured by mathematics; new theories promise to unify physics and chemistry and to demystify the nature of light. As the scientific understanding of the structure of nature explodes in growth, so too do its uses, in the removal of what had seemed eternal obstacles to human flourishing in health, safety, and ease of activity. The fruits of this work grow and fortify the armies of Europe, a busy, relentless buzz underneath unprecedented peace, prosperity, and an extraordinary blossoming of human culture, music, art, literature, and scholarship.

In the fascist regimes of Italy, Spain, and wartime France, political leaders fill the airwaves with a thick fog of lies. The enemy is at the gates. War makes men. A new world is possible. It is expected that the lies will provide the content for any conversation and will shape the choices and form the lives of the citizens. A network of informants relays to the secret police any sign that the lies are disbelieved. Brutal prisons and camps hide the sufferings of the dissenters from view.

In the interwar period in the American North, a young African American man has few prospects. In his childhood his angry and defiant father is murdered by white men, and his family dissolved by the local welfare office. The highest achieving student in his all-white class, he is expected to become a carpenter or a janitor. Angry and defiant like his father, he immerses himself in the hustles of New York City and Boston, selling drugs, procuring women, playing the numbers. He is arrested and sent to prison. He lives in a cell with a bucket for a toilet, his drug habit fed by hustling prison officers.

Naples after the war is beaten down by brutal poverty. The criminal networks own every profitable business. Craftsmen who once prized their own work are tormented by the bitterness of not being able to support their families. Their frustration turns to violence against their wives, children, and neighbors. Women and children whose husbands or fathers are dead or imprisoned are subject to every kind of predation. The past is never talked about, and the future is never imagined. Violence provides revenge, entertainment, consolation. It is sought for its own sake. Even school competitions turn into street fights.

In what follows I refer to "the world" as something that needs to be escaped. By this phrase I do not mean the whole world, the splendid wilderness filled with animals, the entire spectrum of human community with its gardens, farms, and families. I mean the social and political world, which more often resembles these examples than not. The world in this sense is governed by ambition, competition, and idle thrill seeking. It is a marketplace where everything can be bought and sold. Even the most precious goods are reduced to products or to spectacles. Human beings are primarily vehicles to achieve the ends of others. Violence waits at the end of every downward spiral and lurks hidden behind every apparent success. The world in this sense is the human default, but it by no means exhausts human possibilities.

What would it mean to escape the world? What kind of refuge from it is possible?

The Bookworm's Escape

We are only a few pages into the body of this book and I have already irritated you by asking whether and how escape from the world is possible. You want to know how the world can be *changed* so that no one has to escape from it. Keep the question simmering on a back burner. Indulge me and imagine that, for the time being, the routes of change that you envision are blocked.

I begin with the escape of a fictional bookworm.[1] Mona Achache's 2009 film *The Hedgehog* (*Le hérisson*)tells the story of the friendship of three people in a block of luxury apartments in Paris.[2] At the center of the story is Renée, an ugly middle-aged woman of the working classes, the concierge of the building. Renée's middle age is filmed with unsettling realism—the camera finds her heavyset figure, her unadorned face, her slouchy cardigans, and her solitary chocolate eating. Yet Renée exerts a mysterious attraction over Paloma, a twelve-year-old daughter of privilege haunted by the meaningless lives led by her family members. Paloma's father is a government minister; her mother, a psychotherapist and professional neurotic. Left to herself, Paloma imagines a world without competition and, somewhat whimsically, plots her own suicide. Renée also attracts Kakuro, the new Japanese resident in the building, who takes a romantic interest in her. It is a shock to the viewer that such an uncinematic figure should be a romantic lead.

Renée's filmic predecessor in raw middle age is Emmi, the romantic lead of R. W. Fassbinder's 1974 masterpiece *Ali: Angst Essen Seele Auf* (Ali: Fear Eats Soul).[3] Unlike contemporary Hollywood images of middle age—for instance, the playwright played by Diane Keaton in *Something's Gotta Give* (2003), wealthy, accomplished, charming, and still sexy—Fassbinder's Emmi is fat, wrinkled, silly, and a cleaning lady, at the bottom of the social barrel. Emmi falls in love with a younger Moroccan guest worker, to the disgust of her xenophobic children, as well as her neighbors and coworkers. Renée falls in love with Kakuro, breaking through the invisible wall between her and the building's wealthy residents. The love affair in both cases amounts to a real human connection that stands out from their appearance-driven social environments.

The twist that *The Hedgehog* puts on this theme is that this unsettling but authentic human connection has its source and basis in the love of learning. Underneath Renée's low social status and middle-aged ugliness, underneath her public front of crankiness and ignorance, she has a secret: she reads voraciously—great novels and philosophy, history and classics. As her neighbors chatter and posture at a dinner party upstairs, the camera cuts to Renée in private, door closed, reading philosophy alone at her dinner table. Later she is seen withdrawn behind her kitchen in a hidden chamber, stuffed with books and a reading chair. It is her secret life that attracts her Japanese suitor, as well as the protagonist of the film, Paloma. Kakuro, the suitor, recognizes who she is because her cat is named for a Tolstoy character, as are his cats. Paloma, the protagonist, realizes that Renée is a kindred spirit when she discovers a philosophical treatise accidentally left on the kitchen table. In a central scene, Paloma is in Renée's kitchen and notices the closed door to her reading chamber. Intrigued, she asks her, "What is behind that door?" It is Renée's hidden intellectual life, her intense focus on reading and reflection, that draws the other characters, supporting friendships that provide a refuge from the privileged bubble that surrounds them.

The intellectual life as portrayed in this film has four key features:

- It is a form of the inner life of a person, a place of retreat and reflection.
- As such it is *withdrawn from the world*, where "the world" is understood in its (originally Platonic, later Christian) sense as the locus of competition and struggle for wealth, power, prestige, and status.
- It is a source of *dignity*—made obvious in this case by the contrast to Renée's low status as an unattractive working-class woman without children and past child-bearing age.
- It opens space for *communion*: it allows for profound connection between human beings.

When we cultivate an inner life, we set aside concerns for social ease or advancement. We forget, if only temporarily, the anxious press of necessities. Inwardness and withdrawal can have spatial manifestations: the thoughts and imaginings that constitute one's inner life can be hidden, unspoken, invisible. We may withdraw from the world to an actually enclosed space, away from public view, like Renée's secret reading room. Or we may seek out a mountain retreat, a monastery, or a college campus removed from the city, a place that seems a world unto itself.

But it is crucial not to take the spatial metaphors too seriously. One sign of withdrawal into inner life is a sort of insensate stupor. In his *Symposium* Plato describes his teacher Socrates all dressed up for a dinner party, suddenly lost in thought in the entryway.[4] According to the historian Plutarch, the great mathematician Archimedes was so absorbed in his proofs that he did not notice that the Romans had invaded and conquered his city, and was killed by a soldier when he insisted on finishing his work.[5] Later writers gave him last words: "Don't disturb my circles."[6]

Socrates is at a party, in a city, and Archimedes could as well have been absorbed in the mathematical patterns of the advancing troop formation. Yet surely they provide paradigmatic instances of withdrawal. Withdrawal from the world centrally involves setting aside a set of *concerns*—the demands of Renée's wealthy tenants, the watchful eyes of status-conscious dinner party guests, social and political perils, and even necessities, matters of life and death. Spatial or physical barriers are only useful aids to focus our attention, in keeping our eyes and ears from being pulled into some distraction. It is not just that learning, thinking, and reflection require a total focus. There is rather some fundamental conflict, difficult to notice and even more difficult to describe, between the desires to know, learn, and understand and desires for anything else, especially anything involving social and political life.

We might recognize from the combination of withdrawal and inwardness that we are looking at a form of *leisure*, at a way of being that lies beyond work, at a form of activity that is worthwhile for its own sake and that could constitute the culmination of a life. When Renée has finished the work that provides for her necessities, she does what she loves most: reading and reflection. Socrates and Archimedes forget for a time about their social uses—teaching others, challenging fellow citizens, building useful machines. They do what most defines them, what characterizes who they are most of all.

The inwardness of the mind at leisure unlocks the dignity that is so often denied or diminished by social life and social circumstances. Socrates is, after all, a poor and barefoot misfit, but his commitment to an intense form of leisured inquiry makes him seem more than human. Renée's withdrawn inwardness has the character of defiance: she refuses to be defined by her low social status. The defiance follows involuntary failure, for no child dreams of growing up to become the concierge of an apartment building. Yet the power of attraction she exerts over her high-class neighbors suggests that poverty is only one way to be dehumanized by one's social status. The wealthy put their worth in magnificent real estate, private jets, designer clothes, elaborately subtle forms of food. But a human being is not a glass skyscraper or a gleaming sports car, however well cosmetic technology achieves that appearance. Human beings long for, need beyond words, something that exceeds the merely material or the merely social. High status as they are, Paloma and Kakuro are seeking their own dignity when they reach out of their social class and befriend the concierge downstairs.

Intellectual life is a way to recover one's real value when it is denied recognition by the power plays and careless judgments of social life. That is why it is a source of dignity. In ordinary social life, knowledge is exchanged for money or for power, for approval or for a sense of belonging, to mark out superiority in status or to achieve a feeling of importance. These are our common currencies, our ways of advancing ourselves or diminishing others. But since a human being is more than his or her social uses, other, more fundamental ways of relating are possible. These forms of communion can consist in the joyful friendship of bookworms or the gritty pursuit of the truth about something together with people one would otherwise find unbearable.

If there were no such thing as a core of humanity that we all shared in common, we could not make sense of our experience of connecting with one another at the depths. So, too, if there were not something in us beyond our social value in wealth, social status, or political achievement, it would not be obvious why an inner life would be anything worth cultivating. In this way, intellectual life, learning for its own sake, suggests a mysterious subject—the thinking or reflecting person, who has a

hidden worth or dignity. But what dignity is and why it is important are difficult to articulate. As is true of most of the large-
scale questions in this book, I will be able only to sketch out some
possibilities for readers to work out on their own.

Before we even attempt to turn to the mysterious thinking
subject, the human being in its dignity and splendor, we need to
look in the other direction, the mysterious *object* of learning for
its own sake. An inner life is fed not just in privacy, solitude, and
silence but also by preoccupation with some object or other.
Reading novels or philosophy cultivates the inner life of a person, just as would a burning interest in geometric problems, or
an enchantment with the lives of birds. Yet not every preoccupation develops the inner life in this sense: hours upon hours spent
alone watching YouTube is not the same sort of thing as Renée's
retreat. Nor is the exercise of ordinary self-concern through,
say, cultivating a taste for obscure liqueurs, or hours spent at
the mirror trying hairstyle after perfect hairstyle. These activities don't cultivate the inner life, any more than most varieties
of solitary self-involvement. What makes the difference? What
are the proper objects of attention that make learning and intellectual life what they are? What gives them their special value?
These questions are best approached by broadening the scope
of our images and examples.

Images of Inwardness

Whatever lofty happiness man in his earthen bonds
names with the names of the gods:
the harmony of faith, that does not waver,
of friendship, that knows no doubts;
the light, that to the wise comes only in lonely thoughts,
and for the poets burns only in lovely images.

All that did I—in my best hours—
Discover in her, and found there for myself.
　　　　　　—GOETHE, "FÜR EWIG" (FOR ETERNITY)

Self-conscious or aspiring intellectuals are often drawn to the grand image of the School of Athens—Raphael's imaginary gathering of bearded pagans, striding with confidence about a heavenly court, wielding weighty tomes, and pointing one way or another. A lesser-known image of intellectual life, although much older and more common in European art, features a teenaged girl who loved reading. The Dutch master Jan van Eyck paints on his *Ghent Altarpiece* the Virgin Mary bejeweled and crowned as queen of heaven, eyes turned to the codex in her hands. Most commonly young Mary awaits the angel Gabriel in her chamber, sometimes surrounded by stacks of books, engaged in a major study (as in the *Grabow Altarpiece*, 1383, and in Fra Filippo Lippi's *Annunciation*, 1455), sometimes reading a book as small as a psalter (as in Fra Angelico's *Annunciation*, 1438–45). In many paintings, when the angel arrives she is reading the section of the prophet Isaiah where it is written that a virgin shall conceive, preparing herself to receive the invitation to give birth to the king of kings (as in Matthias Grunewald's *Annunciation*, 1513–15).

According to a tradition first attested by the ancient Bible commentator Origen (*Homilies on Luke* 6.7), Mary was learned in the Hebrew scriptures; she had studied the law and meditated daily on the prophets. So she understood that the angel's message that she would bear a son was a part of God's plan for salvation. Her wisdom and learning explain the subtlety and caution with which she responds to the angel's announcement in the Gospel of Luke by asking, "How can this be?" (Luke 1:34). The fourth-century church father Ambrose praises her response—neither refusing belief, like Zechariah a few verses earlier, nor intimidated into hasty agreement by fear of her angelic visitor (*Commentary on Luke*, on 1:34).

An ancient Syriac dialogue between Joseph and Mary imagines Joseph rebuking Mary for her apparent unchastity while Mary rebukes him in turn for his inferior knowledge of the scriptures:

> JOSEPH: You have gone astray like water, chaste girl; just take the Scriptures and read
> how virgins do not conceive
> without intercourse, as you are saying.
> MARY: You have gone astray, Joseph; take and read for yourself
> in Isaiah it is written all about me,
> how a virgin shall bear fruit;
> if that is not true, do not accept my word.[7]

Mary's love of study is held up by the church fathers as a model for Christian believers. Ambrose includes "studious in reading" in a catalog of her virtues, and he explains the condition in which the angel found her:

> [Mary], when the angel entered, was found at home in privacy, without a companion, that no one might interrupt her attention or disturb her; and she did not desire any women as companions, who had the companionship of good thoughts. Moreover she seemed to herself to be less alone when she was alone. For how could she be alone, who had with her so many books, so many archangels, so many prophets?[8]

Her bookish solitude is a sign of her independence, her lack of ambition, her focused absorption in the task at hand. It is emphasized at the moment of the angel's appearance, because the angel's proposal is a challenge comparable only to God's invitation to Abraham to slaughter his son. If we imagine Mary as a living human being, we know that she must have had many plans, interests, concerns: her upcoming marriage to Joseph, for example, as well as her relations to her parents, to her village, and to its religious elders. It is a fact never mentioned in the Gospels that to conceive a child outside of marriage exposed a woman to death or exile. The invitation offered to Mary is to endure an apparently terrible fate. Her inward focus, her love for the words and teachings of the scriptures, enables her to consent regardless of the social consequences of the angel's proposal. Only a profound trust in a goodness beyond any offered by social life could permit such a radical decision, a trust nurtured in inward seclusion.

The inward focus shown by Mary's studiousness is also part of the meaning of Mary's perpetual virginity. She does not submit to the common purpose that her community established for women—sexual pleasure and the extension of clans and bloodlines. So her virginity also secures her dignity, her standing beyond mere social utility. The social world is a realm of suspicion: the locus of ambition and competitive striving, the engine of using and instrumentalizing, the dissipation of energy into anxiety and petty spites. Only in withdrawing from it can the fundamentals of human and divine life become clear.

Thus in the paintings of the angel's announcement from the Middle Ages and Renaissance, Mary is always alone, sometimes explicitly removed from the hustle and bustle of city streets (as in Crivelli's *Annunciation*, 1486), and her shelter or enclosure, her hidden room, is always emphasized. The development of her intellect takes place in private, in the "garden enclosed"; it represents the intimate meeting between the Word of God and herself, where the Word is understood both as a divine invitation, immediately understood, and as Christ himself whom she carries in her womb. So Augustine: "The angel announces; the Virgin hears, believes, conceives, faith in her mind, Christ in her womb."[9] Here Augustine is echoing Paul: "Faith comes through what is heard; and what is heard through the word of Christ" (Romans 10:17). Augustine also is holding up a model for believers. The ordinary believer too is meant to hear, believe, conceive, give birth: "When you believe in the heart unto justice, you conceive Christ; when with the lips you confess unto salvation, you give birth to Christ."[10]

Mary is one image of the intellectual life as a withdrawal from the world to cultivate the inner life. The old fathers might have thought of her as a mere bodily vehicle for the divine body of Christ. Yet to them her inner life was crucial: her consent, above all, to the divine plan, to bear a child, but also her possession of the intellectual virtues—thoughtfulness, wisdom, understanding—that made that consent possible. In the face of everyday pressures and demands to the contrary, she chooses the most important things. Therefore her image was drawn to reflect the highest development of a human being, humanity in its full dignity and splendor, an actor at the crucial moment in the history of the world who was at the same time held up as a model for anyone to imitate.

The image of Mary the bookworm is a pious image, born of the piety of the old fathers and fed by the devotion of centuries of believers. But its resonance with our earlier images of Renée the bookworm, Socrates, and Archimedes suggests that the image has a more universal human shape. Indeed, we find many of its features reflected elsewhere.

Consider the story of Albert Einstein. Judged a failure as a graduate student in physics, he could not find work teaching and researching at a university. He worked for seven years as a patent clerk, and in his spare time he wrote his seminal papers on the photoelectric effect, Brownian motion, and the theory of special relativity—papers that turned physics upside down. He called the patent office "that worldly cloister where I hatched my most beautiful ideas."[11]

By calling the patent office a "worldly cloister," Einstein means that this place of legal business, where a normal employee would go to earn a living in exchange for performing a certain public service, was for him a place of removal and retreat. For someone else it might have been the launching pad for a sparkling career in the civil service. But it is a cloister for Einstein, since in the office there were no hotshot professors to impress, no university administrators to placate, no students to whom he had to justify his existence. It is, then, chiefly a place where the love of learning is put to the test, where ambition is frustrated, where his work has to run on its own power without the grease of seeking out carrots and avoiding sticks. In the quiet of the patent office the beauty of the structures of nature can take hold of him and display itself with clarity.

In his discussions of the threats to real learning in other contexts, Einstein contrasted the "coercion" of academic life with the freedom that nurtures natural curiosity:

> It is, in fact, nothing short of a miracle that the modern methods of instruction have not yet entirely strangled the holy curiosity of inquiry; for this delicate little plant, aside from stimulation, stands mainly in need of freedom; without this it goes to wreck and ruin without fail. It is a very grave mistake to think that the enjoyment of seeing and searching can be promoted by means of coercion and a sense of duty. To the contrary, I believe that it would be possible to rob even a healthy beast of prey of its voraciousness, if it were possible,

with the aid of a whip, to force the beast to devour continuously, even when not hungry.[12]

In Einstein's thinking, we desire to inquire naturally, just as a plant strains upward; to force the development of this desire by incentive and punishment makes as little sense as forcing a predator to devour or threatening a plant to make it grow.

Natural as the little plant may be, the seclusion of Einstein's patent office is not chosen, as Mary's is, but presented to him as a place of failure. While he saw the job in the patent office as a saving grace after months of struggling to feed himself, it is evident from his continued attempts to secure an academic position that it was not the first choice of the job-hunting graduate student, hungry for approval.[13] For those of us without the strength or the insight to choose for ourselves such quiet, withdrawn places, failure is perhaps the best-trod route to inwardness.

It is possible that Einstein's failure would not have been so productive if he were not already accustomed to withdrawal into the world of mathematics and nature. His sister remembered that as a child, "Even in a large, quite noisy group, he could withdraw to the sofa, take pen and paper in hand, set the inkstand precariously on the armrest, and lose himself so completely in a problem that the conversation of many voices stimulated rather than disturbed him."[14]

One might judge that Einstein found in his inner life the resources to see his social environment clearly, that he too came out well in a certain sort of test. Years later, after his work was recognized and he was appointed to a research institute in Berlin, he found himself at odds with his colleagues at the opening of the First World War. Members of the German scientific community rallied behind the government and devoted their talents to the war effort. Eighty-three prominent intellectuals signed a public letter supporting the German government's wartime aggression. Einstein's closest friend was the brilliant chemist Fritz Haber, who turned his intellect to the invention of the poisonous gases that could be deployed in battle, thus playing his part in murdering and terrifying thousands of soldiers.[15] The Germany of the early twentieth century was at the pinnacle of human culture: science, literature, scholarship, music. That it turned to conquest and large-scale murder gives the lie to the claim that higher culture is humanizing in itself.

We might see that Einstein was disciplined by his love of physics to view the breaking apart of the European scientific community under the strains of war with appropriate distress. Moreover, his social and academic failures, including his long isolation in the patent office, gave him a vantage point to see the horror of the war and to resist supporting it in the face of dramatic social pressure. He wrote at the time, "I'm now beginning to feel comfortable in the mad turmoil of the present, in conscious detachment from all things that occupy the deranged public. Why should one not live enjoyably as a member of the madhouse staff? All madmen are respected as those for whom the building in which one lives is constructed."[16] The worldly cloister of Einstein's patent office, then, has its origins in the inner absorption of the child doing math problems in the midst of a party, and it foreshadows the man capable of seeing his social and political surroundings—to other eyes ordinary or even grand—for the madhouse that they were.

Failure like Einstein's is one way to withdraw into the inner life; force is another. The French mathematician André Weil—brother of the philosopher Simone Weil—was imprisoned in the early 1940s for refusing to serve in the army.[17] During his time in prison he undertook a major mathematical proof, the

Riemann hypothesis for curves over finite fields. He wrote to his wife, taking pleasure in the irony of his situation:

> My mathematics work is proceeding beyond my wildest hopes, and I am even a bit worried—if it's only in prison that I work so well, will I have to arrange to spend two or three months locked up every year? In the meantime, I am contemplating writing a report to the proper authorities, as follows: "To the Director of Scientific Research: Having recently been in a position to discover through personal experience the considerable advantages afforded to pure and disinterested research by a stay in the establishments of the Penitentiary System, I take the liberty of, etc. etc."
>
> As for my work, it is going so well that today I am sending Papa Cartan a note for the Comptes-Rendus. I have never written, perhaps never even seen, a note in the Comptes-Rendus in which so many results are compressed into such a small space. I am very pleased with it, and especially because of where it was written (it must be a first in the history of mathematics) and because it is a fine way of letting all my mathematical friends around the world know that I exist. And I am thrilled by the beauty of my theorems.[18]

One might think that the reasons Weil produced better mathematical work in prison are straightforward: more free time, fewer distractions of ordinary life. But Weil jokes about prison's advantage for "pure and disinterested research" and, echoing Einstein, praises the beauty of his theorems. So he too suggests that his work was nurtured by separation from social or political agendas, competition, social hierarchy, objects of ambition, the expectations of others. The pursuit of beautiful theorems might elsewhere be crowded out by things that seemed more pressing but that ultimately mattered less.

Weil considers his prison-nurtured work a "first," but his nineteenth-century predecessor Gaulois also did mathematical work in prison; and, indeed, prison has proved to be fertile ground for many intellectual endeavors. The Italian communist leader Antonio Gramsci was imprisoned for eleven years by Mussolini's fascist government. While imprisoned he underwent a dramatic physical decline that ended in his death at the age of forty-six. During those years he read anything he could get his hands on, and produced three thousand pages of notes and letters that were eventually smuggled out to his friends and followers. He wrote, after he was arrested:

> I am tormented (this is, I think, a phenomenon proper to prisoners) by this idea: that I should do something "für ewig" [for eternity], according to the complex conception of Goethe, that I remember tormented our Pascoli very much. Ultimately, I would like, according to a pre-established plan, to occupy myself intensely and systematically with some topic that absorbs me and centralizes my interior life.[19]

Gramsci set out to study Italian intellectuals, comparative linguistics, the playwright Pirandello, the serial novel, and popular taste in literature. The bleakness of his surroundings and his physical suffering drove him into what he called his interior life.

Gramsci's appeal to his interior life and to a notion of eternity sits uncomfortably with his own account of thinking and philosophizing as embedded in the struggle for power between social classes. There surely can be no value to inwardness as such if we believe that intellectual work cannot be separated from politics. It is true that Gramsci alludes to Goethe's poem "For Eternity" (quoted at the beginning of this section), which suggests that the eternal is found in the here and now, rather than in a nonmaterial transcendent being or God. But Goethe's eternity still seems individual, inward, and beyond politics.

We may be able to see Gramsci's inner life as an assertion of will against his political opponents and what he considered to be the forces ranged against ultimate social and political liberation. On this interpretation, his intellectual work would be still directed at a practical political project—just one that he contributed to in words alone. Such an account fits with the perceptions of his captors: according to an old story, during his trial his prosecutor pointed to him and declared, "For twenty years we must stop this brain from functioning."[20]

Perhaps the most famous and dramatic example of intellectual development in prison is that of Malcolm X.[21] Malcolm Little (as he was born) entered prison immersed in drugs, sex, and petty crime. In prison he met a polymath named John Elton Bembry who was steeped in culture and history, able to hold forth on a wide variety of fascinating topics. On his advice Malcolm began to read—first the dictionary, then books on etymology and linguistics. He studied elementary Latin and German. He converted to Islam, a faith introduced to him by his brothers. In the following years he read the Bible and the Qur'an, Nietzsche, Schopenhauer, Spinoza, and Kant, as well as works of Asian philosophy. He pored over an especially loved book of the archaeological wonders of the East and the West. He learned the history of colonialism, of slavery, and of African peoples. He felt his old ways of thinking disappear "like snow off of a roof."[22] He filled his letters with verse, writing to his brother: "I'm a real bug for poetry. When you think back over all of our past lives, only poetry could best fit into the vast emptiness created by men."[23] He described his time in prison in another letter as "a blessing in disguise, for it provided me with the Solitude that produced many nights of Meditation."[24]

Once he left prison, Malcolm became a minister in the Nation of Islam, gathering fame as a clear and forceful voice for African American communities beaten down by the poverty and violence nurtured in racial prejudice. His profuse stream of public speeches masked a disciplined inwardness, a constant struggle to see things as they were and to commit himself accordingly. So over time he came to reject the anti-white teachings of the Nation and underwent a second conversion to the broader humanism of orthodox Islam. The culmination of the second conversion was a pilgrimage to Mecca, where he saw the stone house at the center of the Great Mosque: "It was being circulated by thousands upon thousands of praying pilgrims, both sexes, and every size, shape, color and race in the world."[25] The change of mind inspired by this vision cost him his life: he was killed by members of his former community. His murderers likely were aided by US officials who viewed the anti-white cast of his first conversion as a threat.[26] Thus Malcolm staked his life on both of his major changes of mind.

Malcolm's inner life, cultivated in prison, seems inseparable from his determined focus on the most important things, his effort to reach out for and stay in touch with reality. So too, as I imagine him, his inwardness permitted a focus on the most difficult situations. Malcolm spoke outside of the socially fastidious, gradualist civil rights movement of the 1950s and 1960s. He did not speak for the sake of social results or legislative outcomes; he did not carefully curate his words to engineer certain effects. Rather, he bluntly made an argument that no one wanted to think about: that African Americans had a right of self-defense against unjust violence. He proclaimed the dignity of people whom everyone wanted to forget, the lower-class urban African Americans who would be left behind by the eventual success of the legal movement for interracial justice. Such pointing to uncomfortable truths and great social and political failures is sometimes called prophecy. Like the Hebrew prophets, he exposed wrongdoing that it was in no one's interest to expose, cutting through careful strategizing for political ends and the self-serving denial of reality that presses us, always, to be satisfied too quickly.

Inwardness, Depth, and the Study of Nature

Our thought bursts through the ramparts of the sky, and is not content to know what has been revealed.

—SENECA, ON LEISURE, TRANS. JOHN W. BASORE

Our new examples have made more vivid the notion of inwardness and what withdrawal from the world looks like. An inner world can be found in an office or a prison cell; it can treat as its object mathematics, or God's word, or the history of one's own people. However, by broadening our reach, we have exacerbated the difficulty of determining the object of contemplation. These human situations may resemble one another in certain ways, but what could be said in general about what these various readers and thinkings are thinking *about*? Mary contemplates the Bible, whereas Einstein studies the mathematical structures of nature; Weil, geometric objects; Gramsci, literature and politics; and Malcolm X, history, philosophy, and religion. What do these activities have in common with one another? And yet the sort of intellectual activity we are interested in does not seem directed at simply anything: sitting on the couch while restlessly flipping channels does not seem to fit the mold. Something about the inwardness and the complexity of these activities suggests *depth* rather than surface.

The theologian and philosopher Saint Augustine writes of the escape that the intellect enables from the private and the ephemeral to the concrete and the permanent:

> What then are we doing when we diligently strive to be wise? Do we not seek, with as much energy as we can command, to gather our whole soul somehow to that which we attain by the mind, to station ourselves and become wholly entrenched there, so that we may no longer rejoice in our own private goods, which are bound up with ephemeral things, but instead cast aside all attachment to times and places and apprehend that which is always one and the same?[27]

For Augustine, our customary life is lived at the surface of things. We seek beautiful or pleasant experiences, or honor in the approval of groups. Intellectual endeavors take us inward to the depths.

Consider the self-awareness induced by a powerful argument on a subject one cares deeply about, the sometimes sudden disorientation that results when one realizes that one might be wrong. In particularly difficult moments, such awareness might reach to the emptiness at our core, where we see the vast scope of the arbitrary objects that could hold our convictions, our senses, or our desires. Or consider the work of a great novelist. In the novel, the most humdrum features of everyday life are connected with one another and made grand, showing the depths and heights of a particular human community, making contact with the reader's own experience, with centuries of history, with anything whatsoever—animals, chemicals, vegetables, or distant galactic objects. These are two examples of the depth that the intellect can open, but there are more.

Augustine finds infinite riches in the self-examination he conducts in his autobiographical *Confessions*. In a childish prank he sees the sin of Adam, and in childhood play he discerns the human enchantment with ambition and with pleasing others. His own sexual compulsions and desires for renown suggest the outlines of social life and how it goes wrong. He is most of all fascinated with the capacities of the human mind:

> Great is the power of memory, exceedingly great, O my God, a spreading limitless room within me. Who can reach its uttermost depth? Yet it is a faculty of soul and belongs to my nature. In fact I cannot totally grasp all that I am. Thus the mind is not large enough to contain itself: but where can that part of it be that does not contain itself? . . .
>
> As this question struck me, I was overcome with wonder and almost stupor. Here are men going afar to marvel at the heights of mountains, the mighty waves of the sea, the long courses of great rivers, the vastness of the ocean, the movements of the stars, yet leaving themselves unnoticed and not seeing it as marvelous that when I spoke of all these things, I did not see them with my eyes, yet I could not have spoken of them unless these mountains and waves and rivers and stars which I have seen, and the ocean of which I have heard, had been inwardly present to my sight; in my memory, and yet with the same vast spaces between them as if I saw them outside of me.[28]

The natural world in its vastness can be remembered, imagined, brought to mind; and yet there is more in Augustine's inner self even than that. The nature of happiness, God himself, the source and origins of everything—all are approached for him in the inner depths of the human person.

Again, the book Augustine writes, the *Confessions*, has itself been a limitless source of discovery; it has been read for more than a thousand years and still draws in those who seek to get to the bottom of things. Readers may use their negative reactions to the book to figure something out, or follow Augustine part of the way and take a detour elsewhere, or follow him all the way and trace out his path further than he did; or a reader may spend a lifetime, as many have spent their lifetimes, simply trying to understand Augustine himself, for his own sake.

Anyone tempted to doubt the incomprehensible depth and vastness that the intellect opens to us might spend some time looking at the work of amateur students of nature. Natural beings, after all, are concrete, external, rooted in material reality. They ought to be simpler and more tractable than the vagaries of the human heart, the infinity of a personal creator-god, or the toothy jaws of an existential question.

William Herschel and his sister Caroline, the eighteenth century's prodigies of amateur astronomy, are fine witnesses to the depths available in nature.[29] At the age of twenty-eight, while working as an organist and music teacher and living in Bath, England, William developed an obsession with looking at the sky. He gazed for hours at the stars and the moon at night in the Beaufort Square garden. He began to read voraciously about astronomical calculation and speculation, and to build telescopes. After five years of following these pursuits, he brought his sister over from Germany to assist him with housekeeping and with his growing astronomical enterprises. Caroline's growth had been stunted and her face scarred from childhood illnesses. She had suffered abuse and neglect at the hands of her mother and eldest brother, and had pursued what learning she could against their wishes. She took to astronomy like a fish to water.

Together, William and Caroline built a larger, more powerful and more precise telescope than any previously known in England, including at the royal observatories. Building it took untold days and hours of painstaking, nonstop polishing of metal mirrors. One polishing session took sixteen uninterrupted hours, and Caroline had to put food in William's mouth while he was working. It was with this telescope that William discovered the planet Uranus in 1781; they built later the smaller, roving telescope with which Caroline found her vocation as a highly accomplished comet hunter.

Both William and Caroline eventually memorized the night sky, able to navigate the stars and planets without charts and to identify hitherto unknown and unseen objects. William imagined, as few had before, the depths of the universe, seeing past what the ancients saw as a sphere of fixed stars to what he envisaged as a vast realm of illuminated emptiness. The Milky Way, even as late as the eighteenth century, was thought of as a flattish surface, as it appears to the eye. It was William who imagined that we see it from the side, that its circular shape is obscured by our perspective, and that it stretches outward into a universe whose depth had not been guessed.

Roughly contemporary with the Herschels, the German romantic poet Goethe was preoccupied from his late twenties with several natural phenomena.[30] His first interest was in geology and minerals, culminating in an essay on granite. He studied microscopic organisms and later clouds, atmospheric mists, and the weather, as well as conducting an extensive inquiry into the nature of light and color. His journal from his trip to Italy at the age of thirty-seven shows all of these interests, containing entries on the strata of rock, unusual minerals, mists gathering at mountain tops, and his newest fascination, plants.

In Italy he visited botanical gardens and observed wild trees and agricultural practices, collecting samples and interesting cases. Writing after a visit to the botanical garden in Padua, he speculated that all plants originated in one type of plant. Over the course of his two-year sojourn in Italy, he found evidence for a somewhat more modest theory: that the foundational organ of the annual plant was the leaf, a thesis he defended in his 1790 essay *The Metamorphosis of Plants*.[31] His interest is what is called in botany "morphology," the origin and nature of plant parts and forms.

Goethe observed the growth and development of a variety of types of annual plant. He noticed that the most outward petals of flowers were leaves, or sometimes partly leaves. He saw that the calyx, the seat of the blossom, was a collection of tiny stem leaves. The petal, which had once been a leaf, contracts into the sex organs—anther, style, and stigma—and these too often turn back into petals. The leaves, first to originate from the seed, originate seeds themselves, as is most obvious in the seed-laden leaves of the fern. The eyes on the stem from which smaller stems emerge are analogous to seeds: an entire plant can emerge from them. Goethe explains the whole of plant growth and reproduction as a series of changes to the leaf: expansion, contraction, coalescence, division, and forward and backward transformations from seed to node to leaf and back again. Each part of the plant is also in some sense a plant; and yet each plant is a single harmonious whole.

In his journal from the travels in Italy, he describes his discovery of the principle of the annual plant:

> While walking in the garden in the Public Gardens of Palermo, it came to me in a flash that in the organ of the plant which we are accustomed to call the *leaf* lies the true Proteus who can hide and reveal himself in all vegetal forms. From first to last, the plant is nothing but leaf, which is so inseparable from the future germ that one cannot think of one without the other.[32]

Goethe recounted his theory of plants in his first encounter with the poet Friedrich Schiller, and Schiller exclaimed, "That is not an observation, that is an idea!"[33] But Goethe himself thought that much of reality lurked past the surfaces immediately visible to the eye. As he put it:

> When we try to recognize the idea inherent in a phenomenon we are confused by the fact that it frequently—even normally—contradicts our senses. The Copernican system is based on an idea that was hard to grasp; even now it contradicts our senses every day. We merely echo something we neither see nor understand. The metamorphosis of plants contradicts our senses this way.[34]

If the earth's movement around the sun is so invisible to us (we still say, as Goethe points out, that the sun rises and sets), we ought to expect reality in many cases to be invisible, available only to those cognitive powers that go past sensory perception.

And yet the *Metamorphosis* is clearly a product of a highly disciplined, almost unimaginably careful, use of the eyes. Early on his Italian journey, he says: "It is the same with familiar plants as with other familiar objects: in the end we cease to think about them at all. But what is seeing without thinking?"[35] We think of seeing as simple contact with reality. But when we see objects repeatedly, to the point of familiarity, they become invisible; the use of the mind, beyond the eyes alone, is required to see them for what they are.

Despite the intense attention that must have generated it, this phase of Goethe's botanical research was a fraction of his life: it was only four years from the beginning of his trip to Italy to the publication of his essay. Even his journals from Italy are crowded with nonbotanical concerns. His botany and his scientific interests in general are scarcely mentioned by his modern biographers, earning a passing sentence or two in the thousands of pages dedicated to his writings and doings.

The eighteenth century was perhaps the golden age of amateur inquiry into nature, and its accomplishments now seem inaccessible, but the depths of natural experience are nearer than we think. Consider John Baker, the author of the phenomenal 1967 study *The Peregrine*. Baker was an office worker in Essex who followed peregrine falcons across his county, on bicycle and on foot, for ten years.[36] The work must have been physically demanding for a short-sighted man who suffered from rheumatoid arthritis. Nonetheless, Baker learned, according to his own description, the prey of the peregrines and their flight patterns, the intricacies of their killing style, and how to assuage their fear of human beings. He condensed the massive journals that he had written over a decade into a single, slim volume, fictionalized as if a man were tracking a peregrine every day for a single six-month migratory season.

The intensity of Baker's engagement with peregrines shows itself in carefully wrought sentences that evoke at once the beauty and horror of the natural world.[37] Baker seeks to capture the bloodiness of nature as it is, without putting it in human terms; but, of course, no other terms are available to him. His only recourse is the discomfort of incompatible human meanings. On one page, he exposes the violence in a peaceful, pastoral backyard scene: "Consider the cold-eyed thrush, that springy carnivore of lawns, worm-stabber, smasher of snails. We should not sentimentalize his song, nor forget the killing that sustains it."[38] Further on, he lulls us into the peace that the outdoors and its wildlife invoke, only to startle the reader with the realization that the scene is murderous:

> The tide was rising in the estuary; sleeping waders crowded the saltings; plover were restless. I expected the hawk to drop from the sky, but he came low from inland. He was a skimming

black crescent, cutting across the saltings, sending up a cloud of dunlin dense as a swarm of bees. He drove up between them, black shark in shoals of silver fish, threshing and plunging. With a sudden stab down he was clear of the swirl and was chasing a solitary dunlin up the sky. The dunlin seemed to come slowly back to the hawk. It passed into his dark outline, and did not reappear. There was no brutality, no violence. The hawk's foot reached out, and gripped, and squeezed, and clenched the dunlin's heart as effortlessly as a man's finger extinguishing an insect. Languidly, easily, the hawk glided down to an elm on the island to plume and eat his prey.[39]

Baker reports, on principle, his own emotions and reactions as carefully as each swoop of the bird on the wing. "The eye becomes insatiable for hawks," he writes. "It clicks toward them with an ecstatic fury, just as the hawk's eye swings and dilates to the luring food shapes of gulls and pigeons."[40] He means no mere metaphor by this: the peregrine's interest in its prey is mimicked by his own interest in the predator-bird. As the book progresses, he seems more and more to be turning into a peregrine himself: "A day of blood; of sun, snow, and blood. Blood-red! What a useless adjective that is. Nothing is as beautifully, richly red as flowing blood on snow. It is strange that the eye can love what mind and body hate."[41] Baker's attempt to understand the bird on its own terms, to get inside the world of the peregrine, ends with his own identification with the falcon's predation, his adoption of what he sees as the bird's love of killing.

The critic George Steiner writes of how we are answerable or responsible for what we take in or understand. He argues that it is appropriate in responding to any work of art or any form of human culture to take it personally, to invest oneself in it.[42] To read and inquire as a free adult is to take on the awesome responsibility of allowing oneself to be changed. If the change were certain to be positive, no risk would be involved, and the freedom to think would not mean nearly as much as it does. Baker is an "answerable" reader of birds in Steiner's sense: he takes them into his being, becomes one with them as far as that is possible. He has staked his life on his inquiry into birds, albeit in a far different way than Malcolm X staked his life on his conversions, or than Khaled Al-Asaad did on archaeological study.

Ten years to look at a bird; three years to see the moving essence of the annual plant; twenty to soak in the whole night sky. It is obvious that the study of nature, too, can be a form of leisure. The Herschels worked for years without contact with a single professional astronomer, without anyone so much as knowing what they were doing, much less recognizing it, encouraging it, or supporting it. Goethe, by contrast, was embedded in a community of like-minded intellectuals, famous and celebrated. Yet there remains a freedom to his inquiries that modern-day professionals must envy. Baker worked without a publisher's advance or an academic department, supported in his work with birds only by his wife, driven by fascination, alienation, and moral fury. The students of nature may seem to be out in the world, but they have turned out to be as withdrawn and as leisured as any bookworm or imprisoned mathematician.

The Escape to Truth

If the natural world exposes depths as rich or richer than the human realm, it too must be a proper object of intellectual contemplation. Herschel, Goethe, and Baker contemplated certain beings: stars, plants, birds. But it is also traditional to see inquiry into nature as a search for truth.

The Italian Jewish author Primo Levi wrote of how work in chemistry sustained him in times of increasing oppression, prior to the Second World War, as well as in Auschwitz and in the occupied Italy of the postwar period. In one passage he describes the effect that the study of chemistry and physics during the time of Mussolini had on himself and a rustic, athletic young man named Sandro:

> Finally, and fundamentally, an honest and open boy, did Sandro not smell the stench of Fascist truths which tainted the sky? Did he not perceive it as ignominy that a thinking man should be asked to believe without thinking? Was he not filled with disgust at all the dogmas, all the unproved affirmations, all the imperatives? He did feel it; so then, how could he not feel a new dignity and majesty in our study, how could he ignore the fact that the chemistry and physics on which we fed, besides being in themselves nourishments vital in themselves, were the antidote to Fascism which he and I were seeking, because they were clear and distinct and verifiable at every step, and not a tissue of lies and emptiness, like the radio and newspapers?[43]

Levi takes the pursuit of scientific truth to be a vital antidote to the self-serving lies promoted by the fascist government, lies promulgated in schools as well as in sources of news and "information." When I lie to someone, I use that person's openness to the world, his or her power of perception and rational judgment, as a means to get what I want. I want a wife and a mistress: I lie to attain both. I want to spend my morning in peace and quiet—I cover over some truth that might spark conflict at work or at home. The personal lie appeals not only to the audience's rational judgment, but also to their own desires: they too do not want to be disturbed by a difficult truth.

The same is true on a grander scale for public lies. As a political leader, I aggrandize myself by exaggerating threats. I rely on my audience's concern for their own well-being and the facts that determine it. I appeal to natural fears of uncertainty and weakness as well as to fantasies of strength. The more successful I am as a leader, the more dependent I am on lies: the vague threat of war turns into a direct lie about the facts of the matter, the unprovoked attack, the enemy at the gates. Words and stories become a means not only to present a false reality, but also to flood the airwaves, to drive out alternatives. The lies resonate and take hold in us, their audience, because they help us to pretend that deprivation is temporary, that suffering is curable, or that a confrontation has vindicated us or shown our strength.

A lie in the service of lower ends denies the dignity of the human capacity for rational belief; by contrast, seeking the truth at all costs recovers that dignity, reminds us of surer footing. So Levi takes refuge in chemistry, in realities that cannot be bent or distorted, against which human fantasy crumbles. Levi describes distilling benzene while a student, assisting a professor of physics. Potassium is necessary for the final stage of distillation, but minute amounts will ignite on contact with water. He removes what he thinks is the last nugget, only to have the flask explode in his hands. A tiny fleck had been left behind. The nature of a chemical compound is a brute fact: its truth may be hidden, but it cannot be changed at will.

How common is a social environment suffused with lies? Is it in fact limited to totalitarian regimes? The French political philosopher Yves Simon argued for a general version of Levi's insight into the importance of seeking truth in totalitarian environments, claiming that constant vigilance against lies is necessary in all social groups. Simon was an anti-Nazi Catholic who watched the excruciating spectacle of Vichy France as a wartime exile. He saw that his apparently extraordinary set of circumstances—a world-historical war that divided his deepest loyalties from one another—was something in fact very ordinary: the tension always and everywhere found between thinking and social life. He observed, "I do not know, I cannot imagine, any group which does not include among its current ideas an enormous dose of lies. That being the case, the alternative is inevitable: either one must like falsehood, or one must dislike the familiar setting of daily life."[44]

Simon sees that if lies prevail in social life and if truth is necessary for one's full humanity, daily life with others is virtually unbearable. What, after all, does daily social life consist in? A disparaging remark about another group; a rumor or story meant to draw outrage; a news story dug up by partisans seeking advantage; a crude expression of allegiance to an institution as flawed as its denigrated rivals. All of these are fundamental to the fabric of social life, especially in times when social life is unusually politicized, as it was in Simon's time and as it is now, for us. We speak to our own advantage: to feel comfortable, to assuage anxiety, to play a part in the struggles for power and status around us. Our purpose in speaking is rarely to communicate the truth about something.[45] In this way we diminish the value of those we speak to; we treat them as our tools and deny their dignity.

Simon predicts our immediate response to the difficulty of facing the lies and falsehoods of our dearest friends and family members: to try to isolate falsehoods and lies and to limit them to our opposite number, the rich (if we are poor), the poor (if we are rich), Republicans (if we are Democrats), Democrats (if we are Republicans), etc., etc. We pretend that others are indeed swallowed by lies, but we ourselves have escaped. We imagine that our social class or group allows us special access to truth.

Accordingly, our focus on truth and falsehood must begin with ourselves.

> Negation and revolt are attitudes which have a certain charm, provided that the attitude which I reject and against which I revolt is voiced at a comfortable distance from my own person. But if I adopt an attitude of saying No to all falsehoods, including those which are manufactured and propagated around me as well as those which I feel welling up in myself, I know that I am setting out into a fearsome solitude, into a desert country without roads and without water. There my dearest companions will fail me. My habits, my tastes, my passions will abandon me. With no support but truth, I shall go forward, stripped and trembling.[46]

Once one turns away from the satisfactions of pretending that only others are in the power of lies and falsehoods, one finds oneself isolated and disoriented, in "a desert country." Simon here describes the poverty that is a matter not of the wrong turn of the economic wheel but of the human condition, the poverty of having to trade social consolations for truth and dignity. This poverty could also be described as alienation, a sort of culmination of the solitude, the inwardness, the withdrawal required by intellectual life. He evokes its loneliness, the sacrifice required by our desire for the truth.

One could also take refuge from the tides of lies and falsehoods in simplicity: in beekeeping, or growing tomatoes, or knitting, or walks in the woods, or prayer. Intellectual life is only one such refuge. But for many of us, even simplicity is not available without a daunting regimen of intellectual self-denial, without a personal, rigorous bout of soul-searching, guided by the luminous clarity of the objects of the intellect, helped by the many human souls who have lived and written in the past.

Asceticism

Zeus, who sets men on the path to wisdom
Who has established the law that learning
Comes through suffering
There drips down instead of sleep before the heart
Anguish, mindful of misery; wisdom
Arrives to the unwilling too.
From the deities throned on lofty seat
Comes somehow a grace, violent.

—AESCHYLUS, *AGAMEMNON*, TRANS.
A. LAKS AND G. MOST

The examples of Levi and Simon illustrate that escaping from the world is not so much a matter of retreating to a hidden space or even withdrawing attention from the outside world to focus on the world within. Intellectual life turns out to be a sort of asceticism, a turning away from things within ourselves. Our desires for truth, for understanding, for insight are in constant conflict with other desires: our desires for social acceptance or an easy life, a particular personal goal or a desirable political outcome. Hence the retreat that intellectual work requires does not function only as an escape. It is also a place of salutary distance, a place to set aside our agendas to consider things as they really are. When we think and reflect, we struggle to allow our desire for truth to prevail over the desires that conflict with truth. We push aside the soft barriers and chip away at hard accretions of wishful thinking. It is for this reason that intellectual life is a discipline: the product of hard work and practice in a certain sort of self-denial. Everyone with even a passing interest in the life of the mind has felt the collision of illusion with reality. The term paper begins with dreams of academic conquest and ends in lowly entanglement with the real problems the topic presents.

The collapse of wishful thinking as it hits reality is a part of Primo Levi's love of chemistry: the experiment may work or may not; the theory of ultimate particles may be proved or disproved; it may be possible or impossible to manufacture a given material in a given way. The outcome is up to the materials and to our tools, not to us. A scholar's multivolume account of the origins of a word or of a particular idea in history may be suddenly disproved, made pointless by a single passage uncovered by chance. A theory can be undone in an instant by a lost manuscript hidden under an artifact in an obscure museum, a set of sentences left in a cave for a thousand years, a palimpsest buried behind pages that we thought we knew. Reality is not up to us.

Even literature is ascetic: we love a character, say Elizabeth Bennet of Jane Austen's *Pride and Prejudice*, but we must face that she is in the wrong. We long for a happy ending to Willa Cather's *One of Ours*, but we know it is impossible, in light of the given realities. So too a work of literature may reveal something about the world that we would rather not know. Upton Sinclair's 1906 novel *The Jungle* threw the veil off the conditions of workers in the Chicago stockyards and showed the inhuman, profit-driven system that produced commercial meat. ("I've been poisoned!" Theodore Roosevelt was imagined to have said after reading it, tossing away his breakfast sausage.)[47] Our desire for a comfortable life, eating our bacon and not paying much for it, is revealed to be incompatible with our basic respect for our fellow human beings or for our own health.

The asceticism of intellectual life is related to what we might call the asceticism of life in general: the cancer may or may not respond to treatment; a woodworker or an engineer must accept the limitations of the materials, regardless of the grand vision he or she began with; there are some stains that just will not come out, no matter how important the garment is; the office can hire and fire as much as it likes, but in the end only the people who work there can accomplish its tasks. The encounter with a given reality, and the resultant crushing of our desires and hopes, is an essential part of being a human being. Every mode of learning is a school of hard knocks.

A Difficulty: Is Oppression Necessary?

Among us English-speaking peoples especially do the praises of poverty need once more to be boldly sung. We have grown literally afraid to be poor. We despise anyone who elects to be poor in order to simplify and save his inner life. If he does not join in the general scramble, we deem him spiritless and lacking in ambition. We have lost the power even of imagining what the ancient liberation of poverty could have meant; the liberation from material attachments, the unbribed soul, the manlier indifference, the paying our way by what we are and not by what we have, the right to fling away our life at any moment irresponsibly—the more athletic trim, in short, the fighting shape.

—WILLIAM JAMES, *THE VARIETIES OF RELIGIOUS EXPERIENCE*

Suppose that true and authentic intellectual life, learning for its own sake and not for the sake of anything else, is found in poverty, in deprivation, in imprisonment, and under severe political oppression. How should those of us attracted by that authenticity respond? Should we deliberately fail our exams in the hopes of finding a way to seek truth outside of academic networks?

Ought we to seek out a prison sentence to secure our dignity, perhaps committing petty crimes to do so if the authorities are not sympathetic to our nobler ambitions? Shall we await the politically dire circumstances of Vichy France or fascist Italy? Must we quit our prestigious careers, taking up the life of a building superintendent or garbage collector, hoping thereby to cure ourselves of our love of comfort and status?

In previous eras such adventures were less unusual. Consider a striking moment in Simone Petrement's biography of the philosopher Simone Weil. Weil has been immersed in the busy infighting of the leftist political groups in Paris in the early 1930s, each with its own acronym, each attacking the other with pamphlets, principles, and ideas. She decides to take leave from teaching philosophy to work in a factory. She spends a year living on only her earnings, and is fired from more than one factory for her inability to keep up with work quotas. Weak, sickly, and accustomed to respect, Weil sees her ideas turn to dust in the grind of ordinary poverty. She wrote to a friend: "I forgot to tell you, in connection with my factory, that since I have been here not *one single time* have I heard anyone talk about social problems, neither about the trade unions nor the parties."[48]

Weil was not alone in her efforts to be poor; many committed leftists of the twentieth century abandoned wealth and status to seek solidarity with working people. John Howard Griffin, a white man, had himself injected with pigment to darken his skin so that he could experience 1959 Mississippi from the other side.[49] The spiritual writer Catherine Doherty compared her own life of voluntary poverty to the pilgrims, hermits, and holy fools of her native Russia, who packed up and left royal or aristocratic families to seek the poor Christ in the flesh.[50] It would not be a bad thing if similar voyages of resignation and discovery became once again attractive, appealing, or fashionable.[51] But that does not mean that such sacrifices are necessary.

Here the example of Socrates again proves helpful. The philosopher Plato portrays his teacher as unconcerned with wealth and obsessed with philosophical conversation. Plato puts in Socrates' mouth the most exalted descriptions of the realm of the intellect that anyone has ever written: far past the objects of ordinary experience, the sources of truth and goodness shine like the sun, and to encounter them once is never to want to leave them. And yet despite his devotion to the intellect and its work, Socrates is a man of his city. He goes to fancy dinner parties, and even dresses up for them; he argues with important officials and intellectual celebrities. He is depicted as always surrounded by friends and admirers.

In Plato's account of Socrates' trial for impiety in Athens, Socrates reminds the jury that he fought bravely for his city in wartime and that he defied illegal orders during Athens's brief period of tyrannical rule.[52] Moreover, Socrates claims that his relentless philosophical questioning of his fellow citizens is a civic service, as, like a gadfly, he stings and annoys them and forces them to question the values that they live by. His willingness to annoy powerful people suggests that he does not care what they think of him. We are led to think that Socrates' intellectual commitments, his passionate philosophizing, and his excellence in reasoning all detach him from temptations to cowardice and compromise, even faced with the strongest incentives to act otherwise. His commitment to the intellect, and his detachment from social life, is revealed when he is threatened with death or exile if he will not give up philosophy. His trial, imprisonment, and execution are his last test. He is a man of his city, but he loves philosophy more than anything: it is the ultimate end that structures his life.

The medieval mystical theologian Saint John of the Cross described a process by which the soul detaches from all matters of sense—that is, all bodily and worldly objects of desire—from everything that is not God.[53] Entering the "night of the senses," as he called it, was the beginning of a three-stage spiritual journey to God; after the night of the senses comes the night of faith, and third and last comes the dark night of the soul in which the soul is most closely united to God. This detachment from the senses is analogous to what I call withdrawal from the world— it involves breaking the connection to things one would normally care about so that they do not dominate. As austere and strict a thinker as John was, he did not believe that actual deprivation of all such objects was the only route to this condition. After all, it is impossible to deprive oneself completely of all bodily or worldly objects of desire. The powers of perception and desire cannot be simply turned off—we can turn the dial where we like, but the instrument goes on receiving. Rather, the soul has the capacity of refusing attachment to them while they are present. If its focus and desire are directed elsewhere, we can possess rejected goods without being ultimately attached to them.

John of the Cross's apparent hostility to perception and desire, and thereby all earthly and bodily goods, might seem bizarre. Why should we wish ourselves shut off? But think for a minute about our initial examples. Why does Renée the bookworm have a hidden room? Why might a bare prison cell or a humble patent office be helpful to us? Why do we go off to the mountains or the ocean when we feel weary and distracted? These are surely common ways of restricting and so disciplining our sensory experience. The senses bring us beauty and joy, but they are also the routes through which empty pleasures, compulsively attractive behaviors, or the trappings of status and wealth reach us. Our eyes pore over Plato's dialogues or geometric diagrams;

they see jagged ice, starry skies, and newborn babies. So too they see donuts, diamonds, Facebook, celebrities in sports cars, and other men's wives. To be dominated by the senses is to be helpless in the face of whatever they present, to be drawn haplessly from one thing to another.

So what does John mean when he seeks to deny and reject the objects of sight? If I am dominated by, say, prestige, I will be restlessly drawn to one prestigious goal after another. The Lincoln will become a Ferrari, the young trophy wife a younger trophy wife. But I could love the Lincoln or the woman on grounds other than prestige. That might be evident if I had known and loved her as the mischievous girl next door, and proved if I stand by her as she is disfigured by a terrible disease. As for the car, perhaps the Lincoln was given to me at a time when I would have accepted any car whatsoever; my admiration for it focuses on its sturdy parts and comfort for long drives. I might in fact hate the Lincoln but keep it because of the joy my grandfather had in giving it to me; or I may keep it as a discipline to myself, throwing a bone to my pretensions in the hope that they will be satisfied and not pull me to worse objects.

Just as having something luxurious does not require that we prize luxury, so John of the Cross maintains that seeing or not seeing does not matter to our domination by the visual. He uses the example of King David, who (as the traditional author of the Psalms) repeatedly calls himself a poor man. But how could the king of Israel be reasonably described as poor? John argues that the poverty of David lies in his will: his will is "not set upon" riches. The pursuit of riches does not dominate him. He has them without caring much about them. He uses them as our detached Lincoln driver does, as a means to an end. Likewise, a poor man might love riches, might value wealth above all, and so his poverty would do him no good. John concludes that detachment, rather than deprivation, is the goal of spiritual discipline:

For that reason we call this detachment night to the soul, for we are not treating here of the lack of things, since this implies no detachment on the part of the soul if it has a desire for them; but we are treating of the detachment from them of the taste and desire, for it is this that leaves the soul free and void of them, although it may have them; for it is not the things of this world that either occupy the soul or cause it harm, since they enter it not, but rather the will and desire for them, for it is these that dwell within it.[54]

When David describes himself as a poor man, a pauper, he means that he holds his riches lightly, that they were not his ultimate end or his dearest possession. He expresses the hope that should he be pressed to choose between love of wealth and love of God, he would choose God.

What matters is the fact about what we love and why we love it. The exterior mode, the literal deprivation, the confinement within four cement walls, the dictator filling the airwaves with rhetoric—all are merely helpful or clarifying. We are subject to gross forms of self-deception. We may imagine ourselves attached or detached, thanks to the appeal of certain flattering images of ourselves, but real suffering is where fantasy breaks down. Physical poverty, failure, humiliation, imprisonment, and political oppression are the hard tests, the trials by which our ultimate commitments are made manifest.

For the Sake of What?

Man is but a reed, the weakest thing in nature; but he is a thinking reed. The entire universe need not arm itself to crush him. A vapour, a drop of water suffices to kill him. But, if the universe were to crush him, man would still be more noble than that which killed him, because he knows that he dies and the advantage which the universe has over him; the universe knows nothing of this.

A thinking reed.—It is not from space that I must seek my dignity, but from the government of my thought. I shall have no more if I possess worlds. By space the universe encompasses and swallows me up like an atom; by thought I comprehend the world.

—PASCAL, *PENSÉES*, TRANS. A. J. KRAILSHEIMER

The account of learning for its own sake as a form of asceticism raises a crucial question. Are pain and sacrifice supposed to be good in themselves? For what, exactly, do we undertake these forms of sacrifice, or to what purpose do we endure the discipline of suffering? The inner life of the people I've described is a negative space, a space defined by what it is not. It is a place away from competition and ranking, using and instrumentalizing. And it is a place of escape, a place away from poverty, drabness, suffering, confinement, boredom, humiliation. It is a place of defiance, of resistance to dehumanizing treatment. Is that *all* it is? So much is suggested by the fact that, say, both communists and anticommunists find refuge there, both believers and atheists; indeed, every sort of person. That suggests that the inner life, even the intellectual life, has no determinate content: it is a human capacity to reject one's surroundings by force of will and do something, *anything.*

But put that way, the account is not accurate. One could reject one's surroundings and devote oneself to heroin, or to video games, and that would reasonably be thought a form of debasement rather than a display of one's dignity. In all of our examples, there is something that the person escapes *to*, something concrete, real, impersonal, and good.

Mary's object of interest is first the stories and teachings of the scriptures, then an encounter with God; for Archimedes, Einstein, and Weil, the objects are the forms and structures of nature; for Gramsci, his political commitments and the thinking that feeds them; for Malcolm X, a vision of humanity and its history that shows him his dignity; for Socrates, an inquiry into the nature of human beings. What do all of these various objects have in common?

Perhaps we ought to think of intellectual life as having not so much an *object* as a *direction*: toward the general past the specific, the universal beyond the particular, the reality behind the illusion, the beauty beneath the ugliness, the peace underneath violence—we seek the pattern in instances, the instance hidden by the pattern. That explains on the one hand intellectual life's negativity, what Matthew Arnold calls the "criticism of life."[55] On the other hand, there is always a "more," never a "less." By contrast, a delusion or a distraction is not a critique of given reality; it does not reach past it but settles for less, provides a substitute.

To say that intellectual life has a direction without a determinate object is perhaps paradoxical. What is the "more" that we love, when we love learning for its own sake? What is the nature of this desire that disciplines and orders all others? Is it like a compulsive desire for money or for pleasure, one that seeks more and more without limit? Or does it have an end point, a final destination? George Steiner argues that all art and thought aims at transcendence, at God or at God's absence.[56] That seems to me to fit our phenomenon well, although there may be alternatives.

In the activities here described, the intellect reaches past whatever is given in immediate experience. That is why mere experiences sought for their own sake (video games, channel surfing, pornography) do not count. But if this is right, the intellect does not provide an escape from "the world" so much as it involves an escape from oneself, one's immediate experiences and the desires and impulses they provoke. Social conformity taps into our desire to fit in; social competition, to be superior to others; physical suffering, to let pain overwhelm us. Poverty and deprivation instill a fierce desire to be satisfied, comfortable, suffused with pleasures. They drive us, as we saw in the examples of Martin Eden or the worker at the Amazon warehouse, to drink and distraction.

"The world" that we sought initially to escape turns out to be in us, part of our inbuilt motivations—not outside us. To exercise the love of learning is to flee what is worst in us for the sake of the better, to reach for more in the face of what is not enough.

The Dignity of Learning

And they'll ask: what helped us live,
without letters or news—just walls
and coldness in the cell, stupidity of official lies,
nauseating promises for betrayal.
And I'll tell about the first beauty which I saw in this captivity:
    window in the frost! No spy holes, nor walls,
nor grating—no long suffering—
only bluish light in the smallest glass.

        —IRINA RATUSHINSKAYA, "I'll live
        through this . . . ," TRANS.
      F. P. BRENT AND C. J. EVANS

The love of learning opens up dimensions of humanity that might be hidden in ordinary life and to which common experiences are hostile: the capacity to understand the structures of space and time or mathematical theorems; the appreciation of beautiful phrases, images, or scenes; the ability to be transported to different times and places; even the simple capacity to reflect, to think, to see through illusions. All these are a part of the splendor of humanity: the growth in excellence of the mind, its capacity to be aware, to retain, to study, or to reimagine the objects of its awareness. The eyes of the Herschels have absorbed the whole night sky; they see differently from other people. Philip Roth recalls touring Primo Levi's paint factory, catching a chemical smell, and asking Levi to identify it. Levi says, with a smile, "I understand and can identify it like a dog."[57] His nose is trained on the secrets of materials and their combinations.

Humanistic learning also hopes to cultivate excellence in perception—for instance, of human reactions or human events. So, for example, the study of literature might enable us to see that we ourselves, like Elizabeth Bennet, have been blinded by self-regard and have failed to perceive another person as he really is. Studying the folly of Athens's invasion of Syracuse twenty-five centuries ago, we might learn to see the folly of a contemporary act of national aggression. But useful as heightened perception may be, its splendor is not in its use, any more than the use of Olympic diving explains the awe it provokes in us.

The capacities of the mind lie strangely in tension with our motivations as shaped by those around us: the social expectations for a service worker or for a young overachiever; the demands made on a young woman preparing for marriage; the human diminishment deliberately induced by segregation, racial prejudice, or prison life. The way that others treat us gives us an image of who we are: an animal to be controlled, a piece of property to be traded, a vehicle of physical pleasure, a rung on a social ladder to be ranked or climbed up on. We escape from these images to recover fuller and truer ways of thinking about ourselves, and thus to find fuller and truer ways of being.

I have already described inwardness as a dignity that shines through external circumstances: Socrates joking in the face of death, Gramsci wasting away in prison while pouring himself out in words, Yves Simon in his plush position in Chicago overwhelmed by the desert in his heart. It is worth trying to get at what dignity is and why it might belong in a special way to intellectual life.

Irina Dumitrescu writes about Romanian political prisoners who taught one another Morse code and tapped out poetry through the walls between them. Some taught each other languages, one using knots on a piece of string to code letters. One Romanian officer in Siberia made ink out of blackberries and wrote out French poems he had memorized in school. More than one such prisoner referred to their time in prison as a "university."[58]

The Russian dissident Irina Ratushinskaya used poetry as a form of resistance during her imprisonment by the Soviet authorities in the early 1980s.[59] Even on the transport train to the prison, at any point of contact with other prisoners she would recite poems, original or classic. Memorized poems were written out and exchanged between prisoners. When she was denied writing materials, she scratched her poems onto bars of soap with matchsticks, washing them away after she had memorized them. She transferred them to cigarette papers when she could, and they were smuggled out of prison to be published in the West. She said in an interview some years after her release: "In a way, it's lucky to have a turbulent life. When everything is too easy, sometimes people lose their love of life, they lose enthusiasm."[60] Her discomfiting enthusiasm shines through in her writing about her prison experiences: enthusiasm for defiance of her captors, for forming a community with other prisoners, for preserving her dignity and that of her companions against deprivation and insult.

Human dignity shines most clearly in difficulty. Why? Why does the act of an imprisoned woman scratching poems onto soap bars move us? I've already suggested that asceticism—sacrifice and suffering for the sake of some good—is fundamental to our dignity. We have many desires, impulses, and concerns. Not all of them are as good or as wholesome as any other. Moreover, the less good, the selfish, the banal, the superficial, and even the cruel are the easier goals to follow. We drift toward them without trying, by default. To be driven by a desire to understand, to see, to learn, to wonder takes determination and work, or the good fortune of an externally imposed deprivation.

The attraction of the superficial and the selfishly useful goes beyond particular circumstances or our individual characters. It is rooted, I think, in human fragility itself, as well as in the disorienting clash between that fragility and our capacities for excellence. We live under cover of darkness. We are born, we die, and, as Pascal says, a drop of water is enough to kill us. We can prove the Pythagorean theorem, measure the weight of light, travel to the moon, and yet be crushed by a blunt object, have our vital insides exposed by something sharp, be melted from within by the invisible machinery of a busy, heartless contagion.

The emptiness and the shortness of life drive us into our imaginations, into the realm of fantasy. We imagine victory upon victory, triumph upon triumph, limitless pleasure without pain. We imagine that death is for beings inferior to us. We imagine that our worth lies in health, or the appearance of health; in pleasure, or in the public display of pleasure; in moving matter in dramatic, spectacular ways; in compliments, in cheering crowds. We think that through these things we have become something different, something not made of flesh and blood, something perhaps shinier and more durable, something perhaps immaterial and ineffable.

I once stayed in a hotel that caught fire in the middle of the night. In advance, I might have imagined that I would leap into action, swinging on a chandelier to safety with grateful young children caught in my arms. "No problem, kids," I'd say, settling them safely outside the burning building, brushing a bit of ash off my sleeve. At minimum, I would have imagined that I'd remember years of drilled fire protocols and do what I was told. Instead, I raged against the fire alarm and tried to go back to sleep. Then I blearily watched my roommate come alive in the moment, checking on the young family in the room next door and shepherding everyone—including me—to safety. Disaster stops us, and our fantasies about ourselves, in our tracks. Our suppressed fragility surfaces. We are not what we thought we were.

I remember being transfixed by Red Sox pitcher Curt Schilling pitching a winning playoff game against the Yankees, his ankle visibly bleeding from temporary sutures. Schilling's is a basic form of dignity: defiance of pain and weakness, deliberate resistance to bodily limitation. I heard once of a mountain climber who lost his forearms to frostbite. He replaced them with prosthetic icepicks and became an even better climber than before. The three hundred Spartans who faced many thousands of Persians at Thermopylae comb their hair before the battle and fight to the last man. Is their dignity a form of delusion or denial, a pretense that they are not made of dust and ashes, meat and bones?

Consider by contrast to our above examples a person who faces death after a long illness with clear eyes, with gratitude, with honest acknowledgment of suffering, without consoling herself with fantasies of future projects, without pretending that her life as it is will survive death, without trying to control the time or the manner of the end with staged theatrics. Here is the dignity of facing the world as it is—the dignity of "thought," as Pascal puts it.

Even the dignity of intellectual excellence, the dignity of Einstein or Aristotle, is not our ultimate dignity. We perhaps all know people of high intelligence who have particular difficulty facing illness and decline. Past the asceticism of discipline for the sake of excellence is the discipline of going eyeball to eyeball with reality, letting our fantasies about ourselves die a quiet death.

Our human fragility might be thought of as a sort of nakedness. Like Adam and Eve, we know that we are naked, subject to a thousand contingencies, held in being by chance or providence. Covering nakedness is as human as anything is. But paradoxes lurk—the cover cannot be totally convincing. We have to remind ourselves from time to time that it is just a cover. No number of mountains climbed, no-hitters pitched, or enemies defeated will save us from being poured out like water or crushed like bugs. And yet Pascal promises us that our awareness of this fact is our ultimate victory over the world.

One could see *resistance to impulse* as the common ground between the dignity of the Spartan and the dignity of facing reality, the honest acknowledgment of human frailty. Curt Schilling resists the impulse to give in to pain; the Spartans resist the fear of death; the honest dying person resists the fantasy that the human will can conquer all. But the virtues of resisting fear and pain will someday meet their match. By contrast, there are no circumstances that the virtue of honest awareness, available to the humblest of humans, cannot conquer.

Further on in this book I will try to further untangle the negative end of the division of a human being, the part of us that seeks the surfaces. But I hope that the positive is at least clear in outline. The mind or the intellect, as seen in the exercise of the love of learning, shows its capacity for knowledge and understanding, for chipping away obstacles to the truth, for contemplating what is beautiful or admirable, even for being aware of the bare fact of our own mortality and fragility.

I have used, from necessity, stories about the intellectually accomplished, Einstein and Gramsci, André and Simone Weil, the Herschels and Goethe. While the heights of excellence are a crucial part of the mind at leisure, they are only one part. The fact is that anyone can take the insights of others into their own mind and make them their own, without a special capacity of discovery. Imagining, reflecting, pondering the fact of one's own susceptibility to illness and death can be a part of the most ordinary life. We are all subject to the realm of fantasy, and thus to illusion; but we all have the capacity to see the fantasy broken up by reality, to see things as they are. Our humanity is not a profession to be left to the accomplished few.

Community and the Human Core

When we focus on something good, or something better than something else, we reveal our own individual dignity, but we also lay the groundwork for the deep human connection I have called "communion." Whereas political and social life is often characterized by use, by the diminishment of human beings into what is delimited by their social expectations, intellectual life opens up ways of relating that are based not on use but on mutual respect in light of a common goal. This may be a surprising claim, given that many of the examples I have presented so far of intellectual life feature an emphatic solitude. They suggest that the authentic exercise of the love of learning either is discovered inadvertently, when we are isolated, or alienates us from our fellow human beings, even to the point of a martyrdom like Yves Simon's or that of Socrates. But the initial example from *The Hedgehog* pointed to special forms of human connection that intellectual life makes possible. Moreover, it was a reflective, insightful, widely read human being, not initially a stack of books, that roused Malcolm X from his hedonistic slumber.

Jonathan Rose's 2001 book *The Intellectual Life of the British Working Classes* collects numerous accounts of the effect of reading and study on men and women living in poverty from the late eighteenth century to the early twentieth. Much of what he describes is the work of grassroots movements; some is the product of middle-class outreach. Richard Hillyer, a cowman's son born in 1900, describes the experience of reading Tennyson:

> The coloured words flashed out and entranced my fancy. They drew pictures in the mind. Words became magical, incantations, abracadabra which called up spirits. My dormant imagination opened like a flower in the sun. Life at home was drab, and colourless, with nothing to light up the monotony of the unchanging days. Here in books was a limitless world that I could have for my own. It was like coming up from the ocean and seeing the universe for the first time.[61]

Hillyer emphasizes the contrast between the "drab and colourless" monotony of his ordinary life and a "limitless world" disclosed by books. But his interest is not in mere escape or denial of the real world. Rather, he describes seeing reality for the first time, as in fact seeing through the false monotony and diminishment of ordinary life. He finds something more real, not less. His mind's opening "like a flower in the sun" indicates the inner resonance, the catching on of the books to a deep part of who he is.

Why would poetry or literature have this effect? Hillyer provides an explanation elsewhere by pointing to the universality of the world of poetry and literature. In reading he escapes his particular circumstances to connect with something broadly human, with different times and places and what might be available regardless of time and place. Thus he describes his first encounter with the world of literature, when his teacher stops to explain what a "poet laureate" is:

> So, for ten minutes, [my teacher] let himself go on [the meaning of the term "poet laureate"], and education began for me. There was Ben Jonson, the butt of canary wine, birthday odes, and all the rest of it. I was fascinated. My mind was being broken out of its shell. Here were wonderful things to know. Things that went beyond the small utilities of our lives, which was all that school had seemed to concern itself with until then. Knowledge of this sort could make all times, and places, your own. You could be anybody, and everybody, and still be yourself at the same time.[62]

Hillyer feels himself expand from a single individual in a particular time and place to a human being able to connect to all times and places. We hear from the poets themselves, often dead and in other centuries; their subjects, too, seem like us in perception and feeling. These connections could be possible only if the writers of the past, as well as the characters, subjects, and circumstances they wrote about, had deep affinities with their contemporary readers. Another of Rose's subjects, the shoemaker's daughter Mary Smith (b. 1822), put it the following way: "[Shakespeare, Dryden, and Goldsmith] wrote from their hearts for humanity, and I could follow them fully and with delight, though but a child. They awakened my young nature, and I found for the first time that my pondering heart was akin to that of the whole human race."[63] Smith and Hillyer have discovered that literary reflections on human life, stories, songs, and epics, are a bond of unity with others, living and dead. Because the dignity revealed by intellectual life is shared with others, because it is a way of connecting with human beings in other times and places, it preserves the individual by marking one out as a member of a broader human community.

Smith echoes the famous appeal of W.E.B. Du Bois to the human bond in books that ignores the veil of racial prejudice:

> I sit with Shakespeare and he winces not. Across the color line I move arm and arm with Balzac and Dumas, where smiling men and welcoming women glide in gilded halls. From out the caves of evening that swing between the strong limbed earth and the tracery of the stars, I summon Aristotle and Aurelius and what soul I will, and they come all graciously with no scorn or condescension. So, wed with Truth, I dwell above the Veil.[64]

Committed to a goal (Truth) beyond what mere social life might offer, Du Bois finds in books a human community open to him in a way that his local human communities are not, riven as they are by segregation and hatred. Instead, on the basis of common humanity and common concern for truth, the dead authors welcome Du Bois into their company.

The withdrawn solitude of the intellectual life as I have described it is not what it seemed to be. The isolation comes from refusing the terms of the social world, diminishment and use. It involves—essentially, I think—a real connection, one not based on use, with other human beings, whether living fellow inquirers or dead authors. So intellectual life nurtures genuine forms of community, as is hinted by the "heart for humanity" and the "kinship with the whole human race" that Mary Smith recognized in the authors and then found in herself.

The human connection that a reader finds with authors, living and dead, also shapes the connections forged between flesh-and-blood people engaged in intellectual activity in common. Rose reports how an instructor who taught prisoners Shakespeare in the 1920s found that the plays not only allowed the prisoners to find common ground with one another but also leveled the distance between the teacher and the students:

> In the study of the drama my education has left me little, if at all, in advance of my class, because the points which come up for discussion are questions of life and character where their knowledge and experience are as great, or probably greater than my own. It seems to me that we find in the plays, and particularly in the Shakespeare plays, a basis of common experience and common humanity which destroys any barrier erected by social conventions and differences in educational opportunities.[65]

The instructor describes a collaborative inquiry, based on one's common humanity, into the fundamentals of human life, with the result that social barriers disappear between inmate and volunteer. Even the barrier between expert (teacher) and nonexpert (learner) dissolves on the common ground of common experience.

There is a simple communion that belongs to all meaningful work. A group of builders constructing a house cooperate in their joint project of providing a shelter, one whose shape and structure create a living space within and a neighborhood without. The builders depend on one another to complete the work. Politics, religion, social class, even personality can drop away in the face of a shared goal. Leisure activities have a similar unifying power. I watched the most recent solar eclipse on the Delaware shore, where the spectacle united various strangers around me—one sharing her glasses, another showing a cascade of

eclipse images through the apertures of a straw hat. So too in the-
aters, concert halls, or cinemas we are all united in wonder, sorrow, laughter, suspense, or fear.

Learning for its own sake shares in this general feature of
human community: it is formed when its members are turned
in the same direction, facing common goods and objects. The
love of learning goes after beauty in words or artifacts, after truth
for its own sake, seeking anything wonderful or curious; it ru-
minates on stored and shared objects of experience. When the
question gets tough at the seminar table, the barriers between
us drop: we unite in search of the answer, which might come
from the unlikeliest places.

So far, learning is like any other work or leisure activity: preoccupied with a shared object, we forget our differences. Any
meaningful activity allows us a space to connect that is beyond
the merely social, the garnering of approval or of favors, the
establishment or reinforcement of authority, prestige, or status. But something beyond the community offered by meaningful work or leisure is offered in the realm of the intellect.
Books, ideas, ordinary reflection on life—these are all ways
to think about what we have in common as human beings.
They can be ways for us to think about ourselves and our way
of being in the world; about human strengths and weaknesses;
about the nature of love or the nature of knowledge; about
family, community, and authority; about the point (if there is
one) of human existence. We ourselves become the objects of
our study, and expertise becomes beside the point or even an
obstacle.

When the mind at leisure turns to our common pursuit of self-
understanding as human beings, through novels or film, history
or philosophy, or by the careful study of the people we know, it
opens up our common humanity, with all of the fundamental

questions and principles of human life. In this way humanistic learning has the power to form unusual or extraordinary kinds of human connection, a power beyond that of ordinary forms of common work or shared appreciation of a common goal. Thus *The Hedgehog* paints a picture of an alternative form of social life, one based not on economic class but on the bonds formed by common reflection on common humanity. Such bonds break the barriers between social classes, between the genders, between ethnic groups, between youth and old age. Our bonds with dead authors or living seminar partners are forged in our common nature, our shared experience, and our shared aspirations.

Factional Literature and Common Ground

The intellect provides a guide to life by its capacity to draw us into the broad transhistorical and transnational community of human beings. Insofar as the love of learning is fundamental to our humanity, we touch ground not only with others but also with what it means to be a human being as such—a broad form of self-knowledge. Du Bois finds in books a social world without a color line; others have found a "heart for humanity," as Mary Smith puts it. But sometimes books also remind us of our smaller communities, of our belonging to subgroups. When I read Elena Ferrante's Neapolitan novels and their account of the lifelong friendship between two women from girlhood, I recognize features from my own friendships with other women, aspects of life that male authors, to my knowledge, have not captured. I have loved the *Autobiography of Malcolm X* since I first read it at the age of nineteen, and yet I am sure that it means something very different to a reader who lives on the business end of American racism, who lives as a hustler, or who serves time in prison.

We know also of jingoist literature, as well as jingoist philosophy or science, intellectual enterprises that exalt our nation, ethnic group, or social niche and denigrate our imagined enemies. But surely one criterion of excellent books is that they draw us into our common humanity and mark out a recognizable human shape. Such a shape appears through and past the specific female shape in the Neapolitan novels or the African American shape in Malcolm X's autobiography. George Steiner describes the work of the artist as the "translation out of the inarticulate and private into the general matter of human recognition."[66] Indeed, such works would be less moving even to their narrower audiences if they did not connect the denigrated smaller group to the "general matter of human recognition": to shared experience as well as what I have called shared dignity, the human splendor we have in common.[67] It is the tension between the human splendor and the social denigration that breaks our hearts in books of this kind, even if our shared gender or race with the author makes the tension more keen and the details more real.

So, too, the best political books are the heartbreaking ones, such as Homer's *Iliad*, where we are made to look at the bravery and goodness of the people who will be destroyed by the author's people. The formative moment for the cultural unity of the Greeks is seen to depend on a river of slaughter, in which the poet counts each dead person, remembers his parents or his bride, tallies his crushed hopes. A modern example is José Gironella's novel of the Spanish Civil War, *The Cypresses Believe in God*.[68] The reader has to watch the slow breakdown of the human bonds between friends, neighbors, and family members caused by the growing violence of wartime Barcelona. One atrocity after another drives each person to one or another side of the conflict. One side smugly neglects the poor; the other hates religion and wallows in personal chaos. If the reader is drawn into sympathy with the messy, human leftists more than with the cold, jargon-spinning fascists, the scope and the nature of the murder they enact challenges our sympathy. Good literature cracks our factional commitments against hard human reality.

It is the general humanistic commitment of intellectual life that puts it beyond politics. Politics even at its best requires factions; it requires divisions, allegiances, the emotional power of us versus them. Without common culture, common commitments, a life chosen in common, even divisions lose their usefulness and become toxic. Like any other set of means to ends, division can be satisfying in its own right. Thus in social media-driven politics, we find ourselves at the surfaces of things, feeding on apparent victories, enraged by apparent setbacks, ignorant of the real-world impact of what we are perceiving. But even when it is working as it should, politics is a competition more than it is a shared endeavor.

The collaboration of scientists across nations has long testified to the broad human concern of intellectual life; the very idea of an international community of scholars, or the Republic of Letters, implies that the community of learning is a country without borders or an army. Even in the seventeenth century, when Europe was fraught with religious persecution and wars of religion, bonds between intellectuals were kept above the fray.

A papal librarian of the late Renaissance, Lucas Holstenius was a convert to Catholicism who fought for territory with Protestants in terms of acquiring manuscripts or producing biblical editions.[69] But his territoriality was at the margin of a broad generosity: he maintained his friendships with Protestant scholars, loaning them books and helping them to find what they needed in the vast and valuable Vatican library. One of Holstenius's guests was the Protestant poet John Milton, who in

Paradise Lost compares the pointless arguments of the demons to the philosophizing of Catholic scholastics (2.555–69), and who dwells with evident relish on a description of the Catholic religious who will dwell in hell: "Embryos and idiots, eremites and friars" (3.474–97; quotation, 474). Milton was overwhelmed with gratitude to Holstenius, writing:

> I am quite ignorant, most learned Holstenius, whether I am
> the only one of my country who has found you so hospitable,
> or whether . . . it is your express habit. . . . If the former is the
> case, then that I should have been accounted by you distin-
> guished beyond the rest and should have seemed worthy so
> far that you should wish to form a bond of friendship with me,
> I both congratulate myself on this opinion of yours, and at the
> same point your good nature in the place of my merit.[70]

The common search for learning and understanding was above the bloodbath, the street fight, the war of words.

What good is intellectual life? It is a refuge from distress; a reminder of one's dignity; a source of insight and understanding; a garden in which human aspiration is cultivated; a hollow of a wall to which one can temporarily withdraw from the current controversies to gain a broader perspective, to remind oneself of one's universal human heritage. All this makes clear at the least that it is an essential good for human beings, even if one good among others.

Learning for Its Own Sake?

> Moreover, love itself, which binds us together in the bond of
> unity, would have no means of pouring soul into soul, and, as
> it were, mingling them with each other, if human beings never
> learned anything from one another.
>
> —AUGUSTINE, *ON CHRISTIAN DOCTRINE*

At the beginning of this book, I asked what learning would look like stripped of its results, reduced only to its effects on the learner. This question was meant to get at why learning matters for its own sake. But if "for its own sake" and "for the sake of its effects on the learner" mean the same thing, we ought to be able to articulate what exactly it is about the learner, the human thinking subject, that matters for its own sake.

When we look at how we have approached this question so far, we find a bit of a paradox. We have not one culmination of a human being, but two. One is the fulfillment of the highest and deepest human possibility, the capacity to understand. The other is the bond of unity between human beings—"love itself," as Augustine puts it in the passage that opens this section, or what I have called "communion."

Augustine says that our ability to love one another depends on our capacity to learn from one another. That suggests that we learn in order to love. If this were so, learning would be not for its own sake but for the sake of cultivating our capacity to love. It might be the only means of cultivation or one among many— but either way, it would be secondary to the value of the bonds we form with one another.

At the same time, the communities of learning described above are not together for the sake of togetherness, not brothers for the sake of brotherhood, but are fellow learners after some third thing or things: knowledge, truth, understanding, beauty, awareness, excellence. That suggests that it is understanding that holds pride of place, the thing that makes human beings matter for their own sake, and that love is something that goes along with it but does not dominate it as a further end. Bare love seems empty or circular without an object. Why is it, exactly, that we love our neighbor, or for the sake of what?

Yet, the solitary excellence of the individual, finally grasping the cause of causes, does feel somehow incomplete. Understanding, like the sight of something beautiful or fascinating, calls out to be shared. The most solitary of solitary learners seeks to communicate, even if only in writing and only for the sake of human beings she will never meet. It is as if love overflows from understanding, or as if understanding were intrinsically generous. Delight in learning flows naturally into delight in teaching.

I have tried to describe what learning looks like stripped of its trappings of fame, prestige, fortune, and social use. It gives us the splendor of humanity, both individual and collective. If it is for its own sake, we mean that we pursue it not because of external results but because of what it does for the learner. But should we understand this effect on the learner as the grasp of the object of the desire to know, taken all on its own? Or is the goal of learning for its own sake rather the connection with other human beings or with a transcendent being—in other words, the learner's connection with a wider community of knowers beyond himself? I admit that I am not able to settle this question to my satisfaction. Laying it before the reader will have to suffice. Learning matters for its own sake, because human beings are essentially knowers, or lovers, or both.

CHAPTER 2

Learning Lost and Found

Action is the pointer of the balance. One must not touch the pointer, but the weights.

—SIMONE WEIL, *GRAVITY AND GRACE*,
TRANS. ARTHUR WILLS

My weight is my love.

—AUGUSTINE, *CONFESSIONS*

Intellectual Life and the Human Heart

The world that we have sought to escape has turned out to dwell within our hearts. To exercise the love of learning in all of its splendor, we must allow it to discipline and put in order our other motivations, by interior war or interior peacemaking. Intellectual life turns out to be a form of asceticism, a cultivation of ourselves that involves uprooting and drying up parts of ourselves as much as it requires sunlight, soil, and seed.

Asceticism is required because learning does not dwell only in rarified realms to which one could travel, as one might go to the Himalayas or to Hawaii. It is a part of the social world, participates in that world's vices, and provides its own obstacles. Our intellectual institutions provide occasions not only to exercise the love of learning but also to advance ourselves in wealth and status. So they tap into loves other than the love of learning, and can form intellectuals for whom learning is a tangential goal. Some corrupted habits of the mind can even turn us against learning itself.

The examples from the first chapter of this book are likely to look rarified and strange to us. What gives them exclusive power to define intellectual life? We know other lives of learning, ones mixed with ambition and success. We are likely to hear that studying the liberal arts is the best route to success in business, as modeled by Steve Jobs or Bill Gates. We know stories of intellectuals whose learning has so alienated them from common matters of human life that they become abrasive at best, cruel at worst. Earlier, I mentioned the semifictional Martin Eden, who through intensive reading isolates himself from every other human being, including the woman he loves. We have also the example of Fritz Haber, and many like him, who have used their intellectual talents for human destruction.

A catalog of examples, parallel to the first, of how intellectual life goes wrong will not be enough to complete the picture. If I am to persuade you that my images of learning for its own sake—inward, withdrawn, disclosing dignity, linked to the heart of humanity—are an appropriate ideal, I will need not only to diagnose common intellectual illnesses but also to describe pathways to and from the good and the bad forms of intellectual life. In other words, I need to tell compelling stories of corruption and redemption.

The Apparent Uselessness of Intellectual Life

We would be chemists, but our expectations and hopes were quite different. Enrico asked chemistry, quite reasonably, for the tools to make a living and have a secure life. I asked for something entirely different; for me chemistry represented an indefinite cloud of future potentialities which enveloped my

life to come in black volutes torn by fiery flashes, like those
which had hidden Mount Sinai.

—*PRIMO LEVI, THE PERIODIC TABLE,*
TRANS. R. ROSENTHAL

To describe intellectual life as useful in politics or in business is
to argue against a prior and much more common point of view.
At bottom, we do not see intellectual life as useful in the least.
We see it as a useless luxury. Why? What in us obscures our view
of the intellect as inward, as withdrawn, as dignified, as a ground
of communion? What keeps us from seeing it as transformative
or redemptive, as central to our happiness?

There is nothing new about viewing intellectual life as useless. The first philosopher of ancient Greece, Thales, was reported to have fallen into a well while looking at the stars and
so was laughed at by a servant girl. The ancient sources were
careful to answer the charge of uselessness, reporting also that
Thales used his knowledge of astronomy to predict a bumper
olive crop, bought up all the oil presses, and made a fortune.[1]
(This story was alluded to in a recent news article about one of
my classmates in studying the great books, who is now a successful investment banker.) Archimedes, reported to have died
for the sake of finishing his mathematical theorems, is also said
to have engineered astonishing war machines for his native
Syracuse, machines that long held off the invading Romans.[2]
We have considered the complex presentation of Socrates,
both a stargazer and a war hero, both a contemplative misfit
and a gadfly concerned for his fellow citizens. Surely Plato's
account of his teacher's social uses is meant to justify or defend
a way of being that seems otherwise pointless, childish, or
self-destructive.

Our vision of the love of learning is distorted by notions of
economic and civic usefulness. I can be more blunt. We do not

see intellectual life clearly, because of our devotion to lifestyles rich in material comfort and social superiority. We want the splendor of Socratic thinking without his poverty. We want the thrill of his speaking truth to power without the full absorption in the life of the mind that made it possible. We want the profits of Thales' stargazing without the ridicule. We want Einstein's brilliant insights without the humiliation of joblessness followed by years of obscurity working in a patent office. Instead of facing reality head on and making a choice to accept the costs of a certain pursuit as they are, we pretend that there is no need to make a choice. Intellectual life can bring you wealth and high social status. We can have it all. So we lie to ourselves that what we really care about is the realm of the intellect, when in reality we would sacrifice it in a second to our idols—comfort, wealth, and status.

Our self-deception about our ends is what leads to the profusion of watered-down, instrumental forms of intellectual life. Our colleges are overrun with attempts to obscure the difference between the value of the exercise of the love of learning and things that are valuable for different reasons. Hence our think tanks and special degrees for thinking-as-entrepreneurship, thinking-as-fighting-for-justice. Making money is useful, and fighting for justice is necessary, but neither is valuable in the same way that exercising the love of learning is valuable. Those of us who genuinely aspire to be entrepreneurs or fighters for justice are thereby bamboozled into thinking that we need a professionalized intellectual preparation. The exercise of the love of learning for its own sake, in the meanwhile, is pushed to the margins and swept into corners. What we in the educational world conceive as commonsense, hardheaded concern for economic and political flourishing is in fact a fog of self-serving wishful thinking.

To make our way through the fog, to reveal the sources of our distorted frame of mind, requires that we somewhat artificially separate out various motivations that usually overlap. Greed for wealth provides one form of self-deception, a desire for social superiority another, and the love of justice presents unique difficulties that we will examine separately in the next chapter.

The Blinders of Wealth

The idling of men is called business; the idling of boys, though exactly like, is punished by those same men: and no one pities either boys or men. Perhaps an unbiased observer would hold that I was rightly punished as a boy for playing with a ball: because this hindered my progress in studies—studies which would give me the opportunity as a man of playing with things more degraded. And what difference was there between me and the master who flogged me? For if on some trifling point he had the worst of the argument with some fellow-master, he was more torn with angry vanity than I was when I was beaten in a game of ball.

—AUGUSTINE, *CONFESSIONS*

The self-deception nurtured by wealth and the social advancement it breeds were accurately diagnosed by Aristophanes, the fifth-century BCE Athenian comic playwright. In his play the *Clouds*, the rustic old man Strepsiades comes from a simple family of goatherds. But the trade routes opened up by the Athenian empire have made the woolgatherers rich, and his family's new wealth wins him an aristocratic wife. As the play opens, his family is threatened with legal bankruptcy, overwhelmed by debts from the wife's high-class tastes and especially their son's expensive love of chariot racing. In desperation, Strepsiades seeks to send his son to the "Thinkatorium,"[3] a school run by Socrates where, he has heard, one can learn to make weaker arguments appear stronger and so win unjustly against creditors in court. The son refuses at first, and Strepsiades seeks to enroll himself to learn the dark arts that can pry him from the legal burden of his debts and so enable him to keep his property and maintain his lifestyle.

When Strepsiades arrives at the Thinkatorium, he finds pale, half-starved scholars measuring the distance that fleas jump. (The method is to dip a flea in wax and then measure the distance from the flea's own footprints.) They investigate the question of whether mosquitoes buzz through their mouth or through their rear end. (The rear, they conclude.) Socrates himself is suspended in a basket in order to contemplate the sun, "having mixed his thinking with the empty air."[4] The studies of the Thinkatorium are evidently undertaken for their own sake—or, at any rate, they are pointless.

At first blush, Strepsiades seems to be a simple man, true to his goatherd origins. The scholars are bent over, looking at the ground as they search for the divinities that lie below Tartarus. Strepsiades thinks they are hunting truffles or mushrooms. The students seek to measure the size of the whole earth; Strepsiades, accustomed to surveying land for harvest and profit, cannot understand the point, given that there is no way to plant or to sell the whole earth. A rustic person, a person immersed in simple and practical goods, may well look upon intellectual life with puzzlement or disdain. The servant girl who laughs at Thales prefers her feet on the ground to looking at the stars. Since a rustic life is a robustly human way of being, it may be absorbing or satisfying in such a way that matters of the mind seem alien to it, impossible to understand.

But we do not see Strepsiades in an unadulterated state of rustic simplicity. Early in the play Strepsiades praises the rural life of his youth, free and messy, when he exulted in honey, olive oil, and lamb; he bemoans his seduction by his wife's bouquet of perfume and saffron, the sensuous lures of wealth. His marriage and the crippling debt it brings forth are what drive him to the Thinkatorium. That is why he punctuates his expressions of rustic contempt with fulsome praise for the cleverness of the scholars. He makes war on his own simple humanity for the sake of pleasing his high-status family and escaping from debt.

Strepsiades is enchanted by the prestige of the use of the intellect. He therefore believes blindly that there is some connection between theoretical investigations into fleas and gnats and the knowledge of unjust speeches and arguments that win in court. But what could the connection be? Restless to achieve his pragmatic objective, he insists on learning about unjust speeches as soon as possible. If Strepsiades were a contemporary undergraduate or major donor, a helpful administrator would design a course for him: the science and philosophy of escaping one's debts in court.

The scholars of the Thinkatorium do not worship the conventional gods—those who protect crops, provide victory in war, or ordain favorable marriages. They worship the Clouds, strange gods who take different shapes depending on those who look at them, appearing as deer to cowards, wolves to corrupt politicians. In this way the Clouds reflect the passions of their viewers: they expose real motivations and character. Their spokesman is the comic playwright Aristophanes himself—the gods of the philosophers are evidently comedians. We should expect the comedy to reveal the true motivations of the characters, and those of its audience.

The drama does bring to light, in the end, the tension between what Strepsiades ultimately values and the new forms of learning. Strepsiades flunks out of the Thinkatorium and sends his son instead. When the son finishes his course at the Thinkatorium, he begins beating his father and boasts that since he has been taught by the Unjust Argument, his abuse is right. Strepsiades is faced with the consequences of his rejection of the straightforward rural values of his youth, his leaving behind the simple pleasures that stay within the bounds of justice, the simplicity that makes community possible. His attempts to keep his family together have resulted instead in its destruction. Still unable to look at himself or examine his own choices, he blames Socrates' corrupting influence, and he seeks to burn the Thinkatorium down. The play ends with the school in flames and its scholars in flight.

The *Clouds* is usually seen as a public attack on Socrates, an accusation that the new forms of learning undermine traditional values. The play is thus thought to have contributed to the climate of opinion that led to Socrates' indictment, trial, and execution in 399 BCE for the corruption of the Athenian youth. But the greater weight of the satire falls on Strepsiades and his family, emblematic Athenians corrupted by wealth and empire. Aristophanes' ruthless eye exposes Strepsiades as a bundle of incoherent impulses. Strepsiades, a rural hayseed unable to handle new wealth and its social status, wants a luxurious lifestyle without having to pay for it, and he wants to escape justice on the cheap while remaining an object of respect and reverence for his son. The "new learning" and its undermining of social norms are more a product of his own desires for wealth and status than they are an alien invasion. If the Athenians did not recognize themselves in Strepsiades, and took the play as an occasion to blame Socrates, then they have been accurately diagnosed by the playwright as blind and self-deceived.

What Strepsiades and his family care about is the acquisition of property for the sake of pursuing one's pleasure, whether that pleasure is rustic or aristocratic: fine meals, sex with a high-status woman, chariot racing with young bluebloods. What does the work of the intellect look like to such a person? If all one cares about is chariot racing, the pursuit of money, and status—or, for that matter, reminiscing about past military victories and vanished rural simplicity—then philosophy looks like examining the farts of gnats. Strepsiades' view that intellectual work is measuring flea feet is the distorted perception of a man who sees only "practical" value.

It is not difficult to see ourselves through the lens of the *Clouds*. We too seek education for material ends, ends that have been shaped by the wealth of empire and the lifestyles it makes possible. When these ends lie in conflict with our other needs or beyond the reach of our capacities, we close our eyes and seek out solutions that seem to require no compromise. In our blind struggle we burn down what matters to us most.

Like Strepsiades, we have lost contact with our rustic roots— our roots in simple, natural goods, in hard work and embodied practical excellence, and in the basic pleasures. Likewise, our anxieties to preserve or advance our comfortable lifestyles distort and diminish our vision of the human splendor in art and intellect, which is the best fruit of wealth, luxury, and urban life. For as wealth and luxury cover over our rustic human roots, they also make possible comedy and tragedy, art and sculpture, history and philosophy.

The *Clouds* concerns just this double aspect of wealth, as both the condition for the pinnacles of human culture and a destroyer of wholesome human simplicity. The play does not show us philosophy in its undistorted form. It remains a joke. But the comedy itself, its stripping apart of the human elements and the revelation of ourselves it provides, would not exist in the unsophisticated pastures of Strepsiades' youth. Is there a way to resolve the tension between wealth as a corrupter of human communities and wealth as the condition for the free play of the imagination and for self-knowledge? Is there a way to win the wisdom and avoid the corruption?

Two Faces of Wealth

Written a few decades after the *Clouds*, Plato's *Republic* reflects the same tension between the human splendor permitted by wealth and luxury and the benefits of rustic simplicity. Socrates and his interlocutors are seeking to understand what justice is by imagining what a just political community would look like. Socrates first proposes as a model of justice a simple, rural community where the farmer, shoemaker, weaver, and blacksmith share the products of their labor. They work to meet their common needs and rest from their work with feasting and song. Justice for such a community is visible in the mutual dependence of community members each on the other, and the devotion of each person's work to the needs of others.[5]

But Socrates' interlocutor Glaucon is not satisfied with this vision of human justice. He complains that the simple men, just and moderate, live like pigs—they don't recline on couches while eating and their food lacks the savor of sophisticated relishes. Taking Glaucon's aspirations seriously, Socrates imagines the "fevered" city that such comforts and enticements would create, a city with embroidery, embellishments, and music, furnished with superfluous beauty and pleasure. Because such a wealthy city would inspire envy, it must also be committed to defend its wealth with force. As Socrates imagines it, beauty salons, flute girls, the arts, and the military appear in the new city at the same stroke.

One might well think, following the history of Athens, that philosophy and the life of the mind enter in with the rest of human luxury, with empire and the growth of trade. But in the narrative of the *Republic*, philosophy—and so intellectual life—does not arise until the fevered, luxurious city has been disciplined and purged by providing its soldiers and rulers with a rigorous education, an elaborate training in physical strength and grace as well as in musical modes that promote human excellence and virtue. Private property is abolished before philosophy, astronomy, and mathematics appear on the scene.[6]

As described by the interlocutors of the *Republic*, intellectual life relies on wealth and luxury. It does not develop in environments where work is overwhelming, but appears only in economies where leisure has become possible. Yet it is not an immediate outgrowth of wealth and luxury. It emerges from a wealthy society that has been disciplined, that fears the pull of wealth and ambition, that trains its young for what really matters. Intellectual development requires a chosen asceticism, a conscious rejection of available luxury. It marks out a way between rustic simplicity and the decadence of wealth. In this way, Plato's Socrates holds out a hope that Aristophanes does not—hope of an authentic way of being human that does service both to simple human necessities and to the heights of human excellence.

The hope of an authentic humanity seems to be worth cultivating, even if the specific form of it offered by the *Republic* is in the end too fantastical or too authoritarian. It seems that we are at our best in both of the modes that haunted imperial Athens, the simple and the earthly on the one hand and the sophisticated and the godlike on the other. And yet, the space where they collide is the space where both characters are threatened, where compromise formations bring out the worst of both worlds.

Instead of embracing the simple pleasure of the rustic and the gleaming insight of the sophisticated, like Strepsiades we fuse the lower appetites for food, drink, and sex with the higher urges for honor, status, superiority, and domination. We seek out the pleasure of eating—a simple pleasure, considered in itself—in expensive restaurants where, given the portion size, a fleeting sense of superiority is our chief nourishment. The sun, sky, and clouds are everywhere, and the splendor of the outdoors is not hard to find, but we will spare no expense to travel to exotic mountaintops and wild deserts for the sake of fabulous photographs, publicly displayed. Our own bodies seem inadequate to the sex life demanded by our glittering surroundings: we must be shaped, plucked, painted, and shined to match, marking our standing in the ranks of sexual status. The anxious demands of attaining and maintaining our social standing crush our hearts and minds along with our bank accounts, so that the truly crucial things seem superfluous.

Wealth has a two-faced relationship to intellectual life, as well as to other forms of culture. On the one hand, it is a condition for it—wealth makes leisure possible. On the other, if it is pursued as an end rather than as a condition for or means to other good things, it chews up and destroys the other human goods. Once again, the challenge is to distinguish means from ends, tools from goals. Wealth is a tool, a means; it cannot stand on its own as an ultimate goal of a human life, not without destroying the other things we care about.

The Corrupting Force of Social Ambition

The Strongest Poison ever known
Came from Caesars Laurel Crown
　　　　—WILLIAM BLAKE, "AUGURIES OF INNOCENCE"

Let's suppose that instead of being an ascetic practice, intellectual life is a sophisticated pleasure. It is one luxury among others.

The country gentleman thumbs through his leather volumes in the morning and hunts foxes or plays golf in the afternoon. The urban hipster reads Nietzsche or Shakespeare over single-source coffee before boredom and hunger lead her to chase down the latest one-bite canapés. So we might justify our intellectual snobbery. We watch art films when the rabble is satisfied with the latest in reality TV. We eat fresh organic vegetables rather than canned ones. We live off the land without getting our hands dirty. Intellectual life is artisanal toast for the mind. (Is it a coincidence that our intellectual institutions end up justifying inequality, within limits—and empire, under the guise of good intentions?)

As Pierre Bourdieu argued in *Distinction*, matters of taste and culture enforce social boundaries; it is part of their nature to indicate social status.[7] But if there is nothing else to intellectual life, if it is only a sophisticated pleasure held in place by whatever supports a high-status lifestyle, then it cannot change us. It remains a form of entertainment rather than a means of self-examination or personal transformation. Nor can it be a refuge when the conditions for wealth and comfort collapse, or if the institutions that support us in our lifestyles fall apart, or if we fail to meet their conditions, or if we are the victims of dramatic political or economic change. (Would artisanal toast or single-source coffee be such a refuge?)

The enemies of intellectual life are not simply yokels enmeshed in practical tasks who cannot understand sophisticated forms of inquiry. A real yokel, as we've seen, is not a simple rustic but someone who pursues wealth and status no matter the cost. We are ourselves the yokels. Inordinate desires for wealth and status are easier for the intellectually inclined to see when they are sought by those outside intellectual life, like Strepsiades. They are far more difficult for us to discern when they become deeply bound up with a specifically intellectual mode of being. The love of learning becomes fused with the love of wealth or status when we view intellectual pursuits as a way to join a superior race of beings, whether that is a higher economic class or an elite superior still.

Among his mostly beautiful and inspiring accounts of working-class intellectual life in Britain, Jonathan Rose reports a few haunting stories that can be interpreted along these lines. The Welsh coal miner D. R. Davies (b. 1889) developed a passion for watching theater. As he described it, when he returned to the mines, he found that his new interests had caused him "to intensify my egotism and inflate my pride," and said: "I now disliked and despised the people among whom necessity had placed me. A better education had made me less sociable."[8] Kathleen Betterton (b. 1913), the daughter of an elevator operator, who won scholarships to good schools and eventually to Oxford, had a similar experience. When she came home, she recounts how she found that "I hated more than ever the ugly working-class district to which I belonged, and . . . even began to hate the people in it—the women with hair in curlers and bulging string bags, the stall-holders shouting raucously in the street market, the grubby babies left to howl in their prams outside the pub. After Oxford, everything was so *ugly*."[9]

The story is, I think, familiar to many professional intellectuals or academics: one takes to reading or study as an escape from difficult surroundings, finds in academic life a path out of one's original environment, and despises one's origins ever after. Following Aristophanes, we might suspect that at the root of intellectual contempt for working-class origins is a love of the comfortable, high-status life to which the intellect has provided an opening. Likewise, what is at the root of our contempt for the openly ambitious, if not a desire to win their status competition on our own terms? Intellectual life, seen in this light, is not a refuge from competition but a more or less devious form of it.

Even within the love of learning itself there seems to be a desire for superiority as such, a drive to belong to an exclusive elite. Consider again Steve Martin's story of his initial attraction to philosophy. He was drawn by the idea of universal, unquestionable knowledge, but also by "the idea that, like a stage magician, I could have secrets possessed only by a few."[10] The protagonist of Muriel Barbery's 2006 novel *The Elegance of the Hedgehog*, on which the film *The Hedgehog* is based, shows a frustrated ambition that her film counterpart does not.[11] The Renée of the novel, for all her love of beauty and books, finds in them an overwhelming sense of superiority to others. Contempt for the unenlightened upper classes oozes from the novel in the voices of both Renée and Paloma. Such contempt, and the attraction of knowing "secrets possessed only by a few," raises the prospect that intellectual life even in poverty is not at all a separate inner island away from social striving and competition; instead, it is ultimately competition on other terms. This may be so even if the terms are recognized only by the intellectually inclined themselves.

If the love of learning is easily confused or fused with desires for wealth and status, how can we escape ourselves and attain our fuller humanity? In what follows, I describe two possibilities: escaping through philosophically informed self-examination, as described in Augustine's *Confessions*, and escaping through the creation of art, as described in Elena Ferrante's Neapolitan novels. These two are my candidates for the transformative discipline of intellectual life and the exercise of the love of learning. I'm certain that there are others, but these two alone might be enough to make escape seem possible.

The Redemption of the Mind through Philosophical Discipline

It is a *task* to see the world as it is.

—IRIS MURDOCH, *THE SOVEREIGNTY*
OF GOOD OVER OTHER CONCEPTS

The hardest thing of all to see is what is really there.

—JOHN BAKER, *THE PEREGRINE*

Augustine's *Confessions* is perhaps the only autobiography in history written as a philosophical inquiry. Even more striking is its aporetic style: in two hundred pages of Latin text, Augustine poses seven hundred questions.[12] They are not all resolved.

Self-knowledge in antiquity was often understood as knowledge of human nature rather than as knowledge of our own individual characteristics, quirks, and proclivities. The thundering inscription over the oracle at Delphi—"Know thyself!"—does not seem to mean "Know what you personally enjoy most at breakfast." It seems rather to mean "Be aware that you are a limited human being and that you lack godlike powers." So, too, Plato's Socrates seeks to know how a human being could be both a fleshy animal, subject to sleepiness, sickness, and death, and yet also the locus of insight into eternal realities. To seek after self-knowledge is to seek to understand the kind of thing one is—that is, the kind of thing a human being is.

Augustine does not deny us a view of the shape of his intimate individuality: his compulsive attachment to sex, his fierce competitive egoism, his haunted inner thirst for understanding. But he is careful to embed these elements in philosophical discussions of general interest and to lead us through them into yet more universal considerations. He suggests that these discussions and considerations have shaped him as an individual, and he describes his life in order to display its general human elements. Therefore the first nine books of the *Confessions* describe his initial enslavement to sex, honor, and social advancement; his liberation through reading and philosophical study; and his dramatic conversion to Christianity. The last four books are the intellectual exercises that his conversion and renunciation make possible: the probing of the human self—desire, memory, and knowledge; the examination of the nature of time; and the inquiry into the scriptures depicting God's creation of the world.

Augustine describes his fourteen-year course of reading as a passage through various ideas and ways of thinking but more importantly, through certain motivations, through affections of his heart.[13] At the age of eighteen, he is passionately inflamed for learning after he reads an oration by Cicero on the value of philosophy: "The one thing that delighted me in Cicero's exhortation was that I should love, and seek, and win, and hold, and embrace, not this or that philosophical school, but Wisdom itself, whatever that might be."[14] Cicero's exhortation ignites in Augustine a restless seeking after wisdom, a form of truth and knowledge that could guide and organize his life. In the meantime, he moves in with a woman and begins to pursue a career teaching rhetoric.

He turns soon after to a sect called the Manichaeans, spending nine years as a disciple. The Manichaeans were materialists who believed that human beings were pieces of reason, fragments of God, embedded in the base darkness of the body. Awareness of the material God-light, hidden within oneself and suffused throughout the world, was thought to be in itself liberating. Material light and material darkness were locked in a cosmic struggle, in which human beings participated and to which they bore witness. Eventually the cosmic light in which humans shared would congeal all to itself, leaving darkness separate and powerless over it.

Augustine found in the Manichaeans images of the views to which he was already committed in some sense, and to which he would commit his mature life more deeply: the superiority of reason to the passions, the blinding and distorting nature of sexual desire and of the desire for fame and status. Such values were commonplace in the Latin authors such as Cicero and Seneca who constituted his education. Yet the Manichaeans also fed him elaborate myths that provided an illusion of comprehensive cosmic understanding. The Manichaeans denied individual control over the appetites—they are, after all, not part of us— and thus Augustine could excuse his felt inability to live without sex. Gifted at argument, Augustine easily humiliated unskilled Christians. He came to be deeply invested in the truth of the Manichaean teaching, which allowed him the comfort of belonging to an exclusive brotherhood, the thrill of victories in argument, a comprehensive if fantastic view of the universe, and a permanent excuse to continue exploiting his concubine.

We can take for a moment the perspective of his pious Catholic mother, Monica. How can Augustine escape from such a comfortable web of falsehoods? Everything in him appears to be satisfied by his life with the Manichaeans—except, we might think, that love of learning and fire for wisdom that was sparked in him by reading Cicero. When Monica goes to the Catholic bishop, despairing of her son's heresy and sin, he consoles her by saying, "Let him alone. Only pray to the Lord for him; he will himself discover by reading what his error is and how great his impiety."[15] The bishop perhaps saw Augustine's love of learning still at work, and understood that eventually it would bore holes in his comfort. Or perhaps he knew that the Manichaean cosmic picture could not be satisfying to anyone for long. Indeed, Augustine does discover his errors by reading. Eventually he finds troubling inconsistencies between the Manichaean cosmic teaching and the many truths he has learned from philosophers and astronomers about the workings of the universe.[16] The inconsistencies rekindle his questioning, and so once again he is driven on restlessly in his desire to learn and to understand.

Augustine eventually begins to study Christianity. He is impressed by Ambrose, the busy bishop who eats only what is necessary and frequently loses himself in silent reading:

> When he read, his eyes traveled across the page and his heart sought into the sense, but voice and tongue were silent. No one was forbidden to approach him nor was it his custom to require that visitors should be announced: but when we came into him we often saw him reading and always to himself; and after we had sat long in silence, unwilling to interrupt a work on which he was so intent, we would depart again.[17]

This image of a busy man able to withdraw into an inner space haunts Augustine—Ambrose has something he does not.

Augustine's naturally skeptical intellect softens to Christianity thanks to reading "some books of the Platonists":[18] works of the Platonist philosopher Plotinus. He began to think of corporeal and material things as pointing to a broader and deeper reality, rather than as constituting the whole of everything. He is convinced finally of Christian truth. The sophisticated and accomplished rhetorician receives through a child's voice in a garden the grace that enables him to renounce sex and be freed from his compulsions. He resigns his post as a professor of rhetoric and seeks out a life of philosophic leisure. (Only later is he trapped into public life as a bishop himself.)[19] Philosophical discipline has prepared him for the grace that frees him from the delusions and compulsions of a life directed to wealth, comfort, and status.

The Love of Spectacle and Life at the Surfaces

And does not the democratic character also live out his life in this fashion, day by day indulging the appetite of the day, sometimes drinking wine heavily and listening to the flute; at other times drinking only water and dieting; sometimes exercising; at other times loafing and neglecting everything, and at another time occupying himself with what he takes to be philosophy? And frequently he goes in for politics and bounces up and says and does whatever enters his head. And if he happens to admire soldiers, he is borne in that direction, and if moneyed men, in that one, and there is no order or compulsion in his existence, but he calls this life of his pleasant, free, and blessed.

—PLATO, REPUBLIC

Every reader of the *Confessions* remembers Augustine's difficulties with his sexual desires. It is less often seen that these lie in an opaque and muddy soup with his desires for honor and status; he ditches his concubine and the mother of his son not for God but for the prospect of marriage with a wealthy woman who can advance his career. (The prospect does not pan out.) Money, honors, and sex dominate Augustine's life even as he draws near to the Catholic faith; they maintain their hold (in his telling) up until the moment of his surrender in the garden.

And yet the most vivid stories with which Augustine condemns his early life in the *Confessions* have nothing to do with sex or ambition. They have to do with his theft of pears as a child, his inordinate grief over the death of a friend, and his friend Alypius's addiction to watching the gladiators. What could be so wrong with a childish prank, grief for a loss, or watching terrible actions without participating in them?

It is the story of Alypius and the gladiators that seems easiest to understand, and that, I think, sheds light on the others. The motivation that drives his friend Alypius to watch the gladiators is named by Augustine as *curiositas*: the same motivation that drives Augustine to love the theater as a young person and that, he judges, bound him to the Manichaeans. Its common translation into the English word "curiosity" has put stumbling blocks before many readers.

In Augustine's account of the human soul in *Confessions* 10, he describes *curiositas* as a disordered love of knowledge, the love of learning degenerated to "the lust of the eyes."[20] He clearly has a specific human impulse in mind; he is not simply tracing the ordinary meaning of the word even in Latin, much less in English. It is easiest to get a grip on what he means through his examples: *curiositas* includes the desire to know about the lives of people other than oneself; the desire for theatrics, to weep over imaginary sorrows; the desire to see a mangled corpse; the desire to look at circus freaks; the desire to see lizards catching flies, to see spiders entangling their prey, or to view the gladiator shows that were popular in Augustine's day. I will translate *curiositas* as "love of spectacle" and hope that its nature will become clearer in what follows.

Alypius at first is dead set against viewing the gladiators. He is harassed by his friends into going, but insists on keeping his eyes covered. The noise of the crowd overwhelms him; he uncovers his eyes and becomes addicted to the shows thereafter:

Seeing the blood he drank deep of the savagery. He did not turn away but fixed his gaze upon the sight. He drank in all the frenzy, with no thought of what had happened to him, reveled in the wickedness of the contest and was drunk with lust for blood. He was no longer the man who had come there but one of the crowd to which he had come, a fit companion for those who brought him.[21]

Alypius's capitulation to the love of spectacle—surely seen here in its worst form, the desire to watch human beings murder one another—is crucially mediated by other people. His friends long to test him, to break his discipline so that his apparent superiority to them is destroyed, so that he will be one of them. It is the roar of the crowd entering his ears that breaks through his resistance and unlocks his eyes. He is overcome by a desire to see what they are seeing. Once he does so, the intrinsic fascination of watching human beings fighting for their lives and tearing one another to pieces takes over.

Augustine's condemnation of the love of spectacle as a disordered love of learning seems quaint and moralistic, but in the end it is not as foreign an attitude as we might think. Surely there are things that we ought not to know about—for instance, the sex lives of our neighbors. Surely also we have desires to see and to hear that ought not be satisfied—for instance, to hear the cries of those gravely injured in car accidents, or to see their mangled bodies. But it is worth thinking about what exactly this desire is and why Augustine thought it so dangerous.

I once attended a popular exhibition called Body Worlds, where human bodies were displayed, dissected in various ways and preserved in a highly engineered form of plastic. Some displays drew me into wonder for the remarkable order and beauty of the human body: the magnificent network of arteries, veins, and capillaries in a human forearm. Others were evidently intended for the sake of lurid fascination: the pregnant woman with her baby intact in her belly, her blackened lungs revealed so that you could see that, as passersby whispered in shocked tones, "She smoked!" Thus, the exhibition pushed past the love of learning into the love of rubbernecking and the thrill of moral superiority. At the end spectators were invited to fill out a form dedicating their own bodies to the (highly profitable) exhibit, to become viewed as they had viewed others.

The internet is, of course, a cesspool for the love of spectacle: videos of lions devouring deer give way to revelations about the dysfunctional families of the rich and famous. It is the bottomless temple of lurid fascination, always inviting us to "See what happens NEXT." The love of outrage and horror feeds even the most nominally serious part of the internet, the news media. The front page seeks to shock and to horrify, as if we prefer to think the world is a bad place.

Yves Simon writes of the ordinary accomplices of tyranny: "Not only did they delight in falsehoods that flattered their passions, they reached the point of preferring falsehoods on trivial matters. It sometimes seemed that, if the choice were to be made, they would have preferred an unpleasant falsehood to an agreeable truth."[22] Nothing could better illustrate the condition of preferring an unpleasant falsehood to an agreeable truth than the social-media platform Twitter. The outrageous, shocking, horrible "fact" is circulated thousands of times, but the simple correction that surfaces later, the evidence of its untruth, gets circulated hardly at all. The love of spectacle wallows in novelty and negativity; it prefers the thrill of the shocking news story, the horror of revelation, to the quiet, truthful correction. So too the desire to see the spectacle is somehow bound up with wanting to be a spectacle oneself: we are drawn into displaying ourselves as we have seen others displayed. Thus, we while away the hours in a reciprocal display with others who are bored, restless, lonely, and addicted to outrage.

What is the difference between the love of spectacle and the love of learning? In a shocking sentence, Augustine describes lovers of spectacle as wishing "to know simply for the sake of knowing."[23] Why would the pursuit of knowledge for its own sake not be praiseworthy? In his treatise *On Order*, Augustine describes how he and his philosophical friends were lured from their conversation to watch a cockfight. This draws them in turn into further conversation: "We asked a lot of questions. Why should there always be fights over the possession of females? Why was the fight so attractive as to bring us down from our lofty thoughts to the pleasure of watching it? What inner impulse seeks realities way beyond the senses? What, again, gets enticed by the senses themselves?"[24]

The thought that the love of learning seeks something beyond the senses, while the love of spectacle is enticed by the senses themselves, explains what Augustine means by "knowing for the sake of knowing." It is bare experience that the love of spectacle seeks—experience after experience, cockfight after cockfight, gladiator show after gladiator show. It does not reach beyond them into further questions or further realities, but is satisfied with the experience itself. It is a form of empty thrill seeking. The fact that Augustine and his friends can be drawn away and remain able to reflect on their experience shows them to be at bottom guided by the love of learning and not the love of spectacle. Their brief capitulation to the love of spectacle serves their philosophizing; unlike Alypius, compulsively drawn to watch murder after murder at the gladiator show, they do not allow it to run their lives.

The role of questions in the cockfight scene with Augustine's friends also seems crucial. They turn from the spectacle to trying to understand it and its hold on them. The Manichaeans offered an elaborate cosmic scheme: a set of facts, or what pretend to be facts. The scheme provides the feeling of knowledge, without laying hold of reality. For example, for the Manichaeans figs contain more seeds of light than other foods; accordingly, wise men consume them.[25] The purported fact is meant to fascinate ("Wow, seeds of light!") and to justify a given taste ("No wonder figs are delicious!"). It is meant not to invite further questioning but to be in itself satisfying. Which fruits have seeds of light, and how many? One might manufacture an account, based on something resembling a principle: perhaps the presence of real seeds is related to the number of seeds of light, so that apples are below figs, oranges below apples, and if the Manichaeans knew about kiwis . . . It is hard to see how the speculative accounts would collide with a hard reality ("I've dissected the fig and there *are no seeds of light*"). An alternative imaginary principle would always be available. There might be no wrong answer, no fixed criterion of judgment, and indeed no honest inquiry, which suggests that truth was never the guiding concern. In contrast, Augustine never stops questioning in the *Confessions*: his commentary on Genesis at the end of the book contains many questions, as well as many rejected alternatives in the light of some constraint.

Natural know-it-alls like myself know the intoxication of the *feeling of knowing*. It is a drive for this superficial feeling that underlies many intellectual pursuits, that threatens to draw inquirers away from the depths of understanding and trap them at the surface. It is surely the feeling of knowing that attracts us to having knowledge possessed only by a few, or to the aggressive accumulation of facts, the collection of a fearsome arsenal for the verbal bludgeoning of unsuspecting ignoramuses. Augustine knew this intoxication well; it describes his life among the Manichaeans.

That Augustine and his friends are able to integrate the love of spectacle with the love of learning, that they turn from the cockfight to questioning, shows that Augustine does not intend to condemn the free play of the intellect as such. Such freedom poses no difficulty, so long as it is or becomes part of a committed search for something more, something further, something fundamental. ("There is but a dim light in men; let them walk, let them walk, lest darkness overtake them.")[26] So also Augustine might explain his own indulgences in the love of spectacle. Later in life he inquires into whose body will be resurrected at the last judgment, the cannibal or the cannibal's meal; or whether the resurrected bodies will be missing their skin, if they were flayed; or whether their hair and fingernails will show centuries of growth.[27] Such inquiries surely have some roots in lurid fascination, but they matter as a part of a broader inquiry into the bodily nature of human beings and into the nature of God's promised redemption of it. The spectacle alone is not the goal.

So too we might imagine that an exercise of the love of learning could degenerate into an exercise of the love of spectacle. Say that I discover through my investigations of animals that dolphins are highly intelligent. I can push past this finding and ask further questions, about what intelligence is or how it works in animal life. But I could also take the fact as the occasion to spin a fantasy of dolphins as benevolent, wise, quasi-divine beings that roam the oceans and bless or curse human affairs. I would be dwelling in the spectacles created by my imagination, just because they are spectacles, and just because they are mine.

It should be evident by now that Augustine does not mean "curiosity" by *curiositas*. We might say that we ate crickets, or took a day-trip to a neighboring town, "just out of curiosity." We mean, I think, that we had no obvious use for such knowledge; we might contrast cases in which we did; for example, "I ate crickets to raise money for charity," or "I went to the neighboring town to scope out profitable real-estate deals." Yet many or most cases of "just out of curiosity . . ." are in fact exercises of the love of learning when the importance of what one learns is judged to be low.

That small-scale useless exercises of the love of learning are not instances of *curiositas*, or the love of spectacle, is shown by their leading to some sort of personal growth: for instance, understanding better what counts as "food" and how others experience it, or getting a grip on the surroundings in which one lives. Augustine's *curiositas* is aimed just at a spectacle: an experience, for its own sake, without growth as any part of its aim or, frankly, its result. Of course, one could want to eat crickets or explore one's surroundings out of a love of spectacle. That impulse might become manifest if I kept pursuing the same type of spectacle: foods other people find disgusting, or strange towns just for the sake of the new experience, as a rambler unwilling to learn and unable to rest. It may be difficult to distinguish the love of learning from the love of spectacle in particular cases, but that is what one would expect, given that each can be integrated into the drive of the other. Each can constitute a basic orientation, as well as a specific desire to do something in particular.

The difference between a basic orientation toward the love of learning and one toward the love of spectacle is that between two kinds of basic restlessness. The one sort, exemplified by Augustine's own journey as he describes it, unceasingly moves past the surfaces of things to what is more real. The second flees unceasingly from object to object, all on the same level—never culminating in anything further, never achieving anything beyond the thrill of experience. It is the bare existence of a human possibility that inspires the exercise of the love of spectacle. The lovers of spectacle seek no good of the kind Malcolm X, André Weil, or Irina Ratushinskaya sought—indeed, it is the bad, the sad, and the ugly as such that hold special fascination for them. The love of learning always wants more; the love of spectacle is satisfied at the surface, like someone scratching an itch rather than trying to heal a wound.[28]

So too it is experience for its own sake, divorced from any further good of life, that holds Augustine in his early grief over the death of his friend. "I had no delight but in tears," Augustine says, "for tears had taken the place my friend had held in the love of my heart."[29] He seems to compare the grief for his friend with the false griefs he loved in the theater: "the more my tears were set to flowing, the more pleasure did I get from the drama and the more powerfully did it hold me."[30] He cries for the sake of crying, for his own satisfaction in suffering itself, not for his friend.

While the love of learning is exercised by Ambrose alone in his study, engrossed in reading, the love of spectacle seems always to be enmeshed in a crowd. The unwholesome community of spectacle, the so-called friends who drag Alypius to the gladiator show, and the companions with whom Augustine is drawn into watching a cockfight resemble other bad communities in Augustine's world. Consider the gang of friends with whom Augustine steals pears from his neighbors for no reason.[31] Augustine is mystified by his own motivations—the pears were no good for eating, and he was not hungry. But he knows that he would not have stolen the pears alone.

Just as the love of spectacle seeks experience or sensation for its own sake, to do something just because it is possible, so Augustine steals pears because he can. He is captivated by his own action, just because he is acting, as if it were an end in itself. This sort of attachment is like being a toddler—"I did it myself!"—only without the justification of novelty. The toddler is enchanted with being on the move, with growth, with progressing from one stage to another. The thousandth time one goes up the stairs "by oneself" should not be enchanting. Doing something oneself matters if some good comes from it, and not otherwise.

The nature of the love of spectacle—that we can become enchanted with action and experience for the sake of action and experience—helps to untangle an earlier mystery. At the beginning of this book, I described certain pointless sequences of action whose goals are frustrated: I prepare to go to the pool but arrive there to find it closed. Now, imagine that I put on my shoes, get my keys, drive to the pool, and face the closed door not once, but repeatedly and intentionally. I keep doing so (I imagine) because I enjoy putting on my shoes, getting my keys, and so on—that is, because of my very doing of these actions. Behaving this way would surely indicate a sort of sickness; if I can't go to the pool, I should do something else. Yet we do something like this when we remain trapped in our endlessly busy, workaholic selves. We work for the sake of money, which supports our continued work. We work even harder, for even more money, which we have even less time to spend on anything but supporting our work.

Work for the sake of work is pointless; it ought to culminate in something further. But it does not feel pointless, because we thrill in our own action and experience. So too the state of character that we attribute to a control freak: I have to make my own cup of coffee, not because I will make a better one but because I am enchanted with my own actions and my ways of doing things, just because they are mine.

We confuse our means to ends with the ends themselves when we are trapped at the surfaces of things. Work is for the sake of a happy life, not work itself; going to the pool is for the sake of swimming, not for going through the motions of getting there; making a cup of coffee is for the sake of having coffee to drink, and we might do better to allow someone else to make it for us.

In Dante's *Inferno*, Dante meets Ulysses, who tells him about his last voyage. After his homecoming from Troy, Ulysses sets out again and dedicates the rest of his life to voyaging, dying near the edge of the world.[32] His condemnation to a deep circle of hell is puzzling, until we reflect on the strangeness of his choice. The lengthy travels that constitute his homecoming (told in Homer's *Odyssey*), diverting and spectacular as they were, might also have been an occasion for growth: healing from the wounds of war, a preparation for homecoming, a search for a kind of wisdom. Such are the goods that traveling serves: growth, healing, understanding, awe at something greater than oneself—not experience for its own sake. For Ulysses to leave behind his wife, son, and aging father to set out again is madness; there is no point to it beyond the experience alone. So he appeals to his men to push past to the edge of the world and to their deaths for the sake of *esperïenza*, since the time given to the senses is short.[33] His endeavor and his leadership are driven by the love of spectacle. But while spectacles are useful for raising questions, for opening up forms of inquiry, or for resting in awe at something beyond oneself, they are not ends in themselves. He abandons his family and dies for the sake of a few thrilling moments at the surfaces of things.

When we act wholesomely we reach for something beyond, something more. We reach past the artificially induced tears of the theatrical production for wisdom about life, past sensual pleasure to intimacy with another human being, past grief over a loss to gratitude and renewal of purpose. That is how human beings are meant to function, how things work when all is going well. Unless we treasure something beyond our own bare experience, we cannot distinguish gazing at a mighty river from gazing at the TV channels changing one to the other, over and over again.

There is still a mystery in the role of the crowd, the gang, the band of brothers without which, according to Augustine, the means to ends, the surfaces of things, have no hold on us. It is as if our love of acting for its own sake is tied up with another's love of a spectacle. Each gang member steals pears and relishes the spectacle of the others stealing pears. The false pals revel and cheer in the gladiators and love to drag someone else into the revel. We want to make coffee our way and we want others to know it. Even solitary channel surfing—and certainly the compulsive use of social media—is a screwed-up longing for communion. We want to stay at the surface *with others*.

In the supremely shallow realm of acting for the sake of acting and a preoccupation with spectacle, growth is impossible. All that lies there is an endless, repeated sequence of increasingly joyless thrills. Our sense of emptiness and lack of satisfaction are signs that we have not in fact attained any human goods or actually connected with other human beings. The dissatisfaction is a sign that we long to attain real goods, and that we long to bond with others in truth, in the depths, and not remain at the surface of things.

The Virtue of Seriousness

τὰ σπουδαῖα μελέτα.

Pay attention to the important things.

—SOLON OF ATHENS

Augustine contrasts the person who is *curiosus* with the person who is *studiosus*.[34] Scholars translate the latter term as "studious"—but this strikes me as misleading. To us, the "curious" person might seem to be the person who loves learning in spontaneous freedom, and the "studious" person an achievement-driven bore. But we know by now that the person governed by *curiositas* is more like one addicted to violent video games, and we might guess that the serious person is one who, like Augustine, restlessly pushes for the better, the truer, the more profound.

I understand the virtue of seriousness to be a desire to seek out what is most important, to get to the bottom of things, to stay focused on what matters. Whereas the lover of spectacle skims over the surfaces of things and is satisfied with mere images and feelings, the serious person looks for depth, reaches for more, longs for reality. To be serious is to ponder one's dissatisfactions, to discern better from worse, the possible from the impossible. A serious person wants what is best and most true for himself or herself.

The contrast between the lover of spectacle and the serious person must not be misunderstood. To be serious is not to have a furrowed brow, to eschew laughter, or even to adopt the grandiose posture of previous generations of seekers of truth. Jacques Maritain met his future wife, Raïssa, their first year at the Sorbonne. They made a pact that if they could not discover the meaning of life within one year, they would commit suicide. (Fortunately, they discovered it on schedule, and survived.)[35] To be serious is not to sense the weight of the world on one's shoulders at every living minute. It is simply to be oriented by the important things, to keep one's mind in a general way on what really matters. It is a call to the healthy preservation of basic sanity, not an urge toward ponderous sobriety.

To understand the virtue of seriousness, we must understand its fundamental restlessness. If we return to the moment when Augustine is enmeshed in the Manichaeans, we may now see something that we passed over too quickly. Augustine has his concubine, with a clean conscience; he can leave her for the marriage that will seal his career, knowing that his flesh has a mind of its own and cannot be controlled by the God-fragment of his reason. His pride is satisfied by the sense of possessing knowledge known only to a few, and by his victories in debate; his love of spectacle is satisfied by elaborate cosmic myths. His satisfaction is apparently total. How does he escape all this?

The inconsistencies between the cosmic myths and what he knows to be true about the universe are his liberators. But why should they break him free? Surely he could keep the concubine or the wife, keep the career, keep his sense of superiority, and simply modify his worldview. It seems rather that the desire for truth is fundamental to him. His other pursuits are satisfying because they rest on something that seems true. Once the Manichaean worldview falls apart, his other satisfactions turn cold: he has lost his excuse for his sexual exploitation, and his victories in argument, based on utter falsehoods, turn out to be merely apparent triumphs. He has not just lost a belief or a number of beliefs. He has lost a basic orientation, a way of ordering and understanding his wants and his goals. The love of spectacle seems to satisfy the love of truth; but if the spectacles lose their plausibility, like a theater production gone wrong, reality breaks through.

Augustine describes the ultimate desire of human beings as not just for truth, nor for any old pleasure, but for pleasure in the truth.[36] Since God is truth, in God lies our happiness. We all desire happiness, and we all know that we desire it; but we do not all at bottom pursue joy in the truth, so we do not all pursue God.

We seek joy in honor or in power, in pleasure or in superstition, instead of in the things that will enable us to flourish.

When Augustine says that happiness is joy in the truth, he means not necessarily the simple truth of facts but the truth about the most important things. It might be difficult to reach the truth that is God from any assemblage of facts—from facts about whales, for instance, or facts about the history of baseball. Our successful pursuit of happiness requires a desire for truth, but especially a desire for the truth about life, desire for the truth that matters most. So too the virtue of seriousness seems closely bound both with the love of learning and with the desire for happiness.

Augustine's love of learning pulls everything else behind it in the end, changing the way he relates to women, changing the way he relates to the status competitions he was enthralled with. It is not one desire among others but a force of integration, a source of a kind of wholeness. His satisfactions are no longer a laundry list but lie in a certain order. His love of spectacle leads to questioning. His love of honor and position is internalized into a personal aspiration to know, to understand, and to be chosen by God. Just as truth undermines his whole life as a Manichaean, so too it provides structure to his whole life as a Christian. It is as if the change in one part makes all the others fall into place.

Suppose there is no God, and so seeking truth will not lead us to him. Or suppose God is not good—and so the truth will not give us joy. Suppose the truth is that we are floating on an island of lava, everything that we care about subject at any moment to total dissolution. Philosophers sometimes imagine that they would prefer a life of illusion under such circumstances. A life of illusion, a life plugged into a cyberworld in which everything goes our way, might be a practical choice, a form of medication or a way of coping with an unbearable reality. But it would not, I warrant, provide a human life that anyone would aspire to. We would not choose it in our imaginations as a glorious or admirable life. At bottom we want to *be* a certain sort of person, not just to seem to ourselves to be that sort of person. Cyberlife would be a human life without depth, a life at the surfaces, a life in which we may as well revive the gladiator shows and devote ourselves to the thrill of watching them—especially since no one will really be murdered.

If we love truth so much, if our happiness consists in joy in it, then why aren't we all happy? Why are the surfaces appealing at all? Augustine points to our aversion to the truth about ourselves. Certainly it seems that the cost of truth holds us back. I once asked one of my students why, at gatherings, students would sooner look at their phones than talk to one another. "Oh," he said, "it's so much easier not to engage!" Encounter involves a risk. It provides inevitable, constant pain as the price for its real satisfactions.

The pain of truth also explains why we might lose our joy in the truth. Having seriously sought out a good life, and having found it, we still lapse into busy listlessness, acting for the sake of acting, experiencing for the sake of experiencing. The ancient monks called this condition *acedia*; the word's common translation, "sloth," hides the fact that hyperactivity is as common if not more common a manifestation than loafing on the couch.[37] We lose our joy in the truth, our focus on the most important things. But, as Thomas Aquinas points out in his discussion of acedia, "no one can long endure sadness without joy," and thus we pull away from the saddening thing and seek out joy elsewhere.[38] We fall into the pursuit of spectacles, whether the spectacles of our own actions or the spectacles available to us from the view of the easy chair. A recommitment to what we most care about is needed: the end of learning, or of service, or of worship. Simple, effective activities (knitting, cooking, chopping wood, the persistent execution of our daily duties) can reacclimate us to the regular hard knocks of the real world.

Augustine's virtue of seriousness, we find, is of key value in our understanding of intellectual life. Intellectual life involves a direction, as suggested above—it draws us on to something more, and then something more, until (and if) we reach a point where there is no "more." We end our striving either at God or at the abyss where God's absence is. Augustine himself, by his own description, as well as Malcolm X or the fictional Lila Cerullo we are about to meet, is a human being drawn inexorably toward the more—more reality, more depth, more understanding. The virtue of seriousness, the habitual pursuit of learning, turns out to be ordered by a desire for what matters most.

If we share Augustine's confidence that our desire for truth and our ultimate well-being will not come into conflict, what matters most for us will make us flourish. That is because God is the source of truth and goodness, the ultimate destination of our desires to know and to be happy. But, oddly enough, a sort of flourishing can also emerge at the face of the abyss where God's absence is.

My example of flourishing in friendship at the edge of the abyss will come from Elena Ferrante's Neapolitan novels. Whereas the *Confessions* shows us the transformative discipline of the philosophical search for truth, the Neapolitan novels show instead the discipline of striving for depth and reality through works of art and exercises of creativity. There is surely also a pious form of flourishing through art and an abyss-centered form of flourishing through philosophy, but my readers can work these out for themselves.

Redemption through the Work of Art

For poetry makes nothing happen: it survives
In the valley of its making where executives
Would never want to tamper, flows on south
From ranches of isolation and the busy griefs,
Raw towns that we believe and die in; it survives,
A way of happening, a mouth.

—W. H. AUDEN, "IN MEMORY OF W. B. YEATS"

Elena Ferrante's broad and deep Neapolitan novels consist partly of a meditation on the relation between intellectual life and ambition, the love of learning on the one hand and the striving for social advancement on the other. They take place against the background of the bleakness and violence of postindustrial urban poverty—in this case, the poverty of postwar Naples. The human diminishment in this community is as unbearable as its origins are obscure. The escape route through the educational system also involves diminishment, a flight into superficiality and self-advancement. But the exercise of the love of learning (as I see it) survives like a quiet flame, nurtured only in the friendship between the two main characters and their jointly undertaken creative and artistic endeavors. Its beauty survives in a universe seen as violent, chaotic, and indifferent to human interests.

The narrator of the novels (Elena Greco, often called Lenù for short) describes growing up in their poor, violent Naples neighborhood. She and her friend Lila Cerullo both excel in school. Permitted to stay on in school, Elena follows intellectual pursuits out of the neighborhood and into a marriage with a middle-class professor and into a career as a well-known writer and novelist. Lila, although on Lenù's account a greater intellectual talent, leaves school after fifth grade. She marries as a teenager and becomes the property of a violent abuser from their neighborhood. She escapes to work in a sausage factory almost as dangerous and demeaning. Escaping again, she returns to the neighborhood and founds a technology business. The different trajectories of the two women, their divergences and points of contact, provide a wealth of luminous examples of how social ambition and intellectual life intersect.

School for the children of their neighborhood is presented at first and primarily as a locus of cutthroat competition and struggle for power and status, street fighting through other means. One of the earliest scenes in the first novel is the semiannual competition between different classrooms, to display which students and which teachers are the best. Maestra Oliviero, the teacher of Elena and Lila, enjoys the competition: "Our teacher, in permanent conflict with her colleagues, with whom she sometimes seemed near to coming to blows, used Lila and me as the blazing proof of how good she was."[39] The school competition between the students, which is tense and heated, involves the characters whose lives are most intertwined over the course of the four novels: Lila, Lenù, Nino, Enzo, and Alfonso Carracci. It culminates in Lila's harsh and decisive victory and a rock-throwing war afterward between the boys and the girls, in which both Lila and Enzo are injured.

Lenù herself shows few impulses to violence—she prefers to hide behind a veneer of blond curls and sweetness—but she plays to win all the same. She is less of a street fighter than a social climber. Indeed, in the novels it appears at a first glance that she is merely competitive, a pretender to higher things without any intellectual drive of her own. Throughout her long journey through school in the first two books, she never describes herself ruminating over a fundamental question or trembling with awe at a discovery. She is accomplished at the use of the intellect, but shows no love of learning. Rather, she relates to the reader every score in every subject in school, each special attention or note of praise from a teacher, and how she compares to her nearest rivals. Her ranking neatly tracks her sense of well-being.

> I passed both tests with all tens, the highest marks; Lila got her diploma with nines and an eight in arithmetic.

> These were desolate days. . . . Alfonso Carracci was promoted with an average of eight, Gigliola Spagnuolo was promoted with an average of seven, and I had all sixes and a four in Latin.

> I passed the exams at the end of middle school with eights and a nine in Italian and nine in Latin. I was the best in the school, better than Alfonso, who had an average of eight, and much better than Gino.

> During that period I felt strong. At school I acquitted myself perfectly, I told Maestra Oliviero about my successes and she praised me.

> I was promoted with nines in all my subjects.

> I was promoted to the third year with all tens.[40]

As Lenù moves from school to high school and university, the interest in scores and comparisons drops away, but a concern with keeping up appearances by saying the right words and phrases takes over. School rankings give way to further ranks of social advancement; being the best in her low-status community becomes her path to a higher rung of a broader social hierarchy. This movement upward through the skillful use of empty talk stretches through the second and third novels of the quartet, and it seems deeply connected with her love for Nino Sarratore, a social climber (and sexual predator, as it turns out) whom she has known since childhood. On the one hand, Nino is a purely status-driven intellectual, ingratiating himself with anyone who might advance him. On the other hand, he is the only character who truly escapes from their Naples neighborhood.

In the environment of the 1960s in which the next stage of her education takes place, the high-status intellectual focus is overwhelmingly political. Talking with Lenù at Lila's wedding, Nino presents to her the empty political speechmaking that will help them both out of poverty. In a bitter irony echoed throughout the novels, Nino's speech is about poverty and stresses the importance of leaving behind "vague words" for concrete discussion of problems and solutions. He concludes with an attack on literature, the study and writing of novels, as irrelevant to the concerns of working people: "Too many gallant novels, Lenù, make a Don Quixote; but here in Naples we, with all due respect to Don Quixote, have no need to tilt against windmills, it's only wasted courage: we need people who know how the mills work and will make them work."[41]

At the time, Lenù is drawn in, overwhelmed by Nino's cleverness and eloquence. Over the course of the novels it becomes evident that Nino has it backward: it is the activists who engage in games of words, and the novelist who finds meaning and what counts for hope.

Ambition and the Work of Art

The old philosophers imagine what the life of the wise will be in the Islands of the Blest, that they will be free from every care, needing none of the necessities of life, and with nothing else to do but to spend all their time on learning and inquiring in the study of nature. We on the other hand see not only the delight of a happy life but also the solace of misfortune; hence many when they were in the power of enemies or tyrants, many in prison, many in exile, have solaced their sorrow with the pursuit of learning.

—CICERO, *ABOUT THE ENDS OF GOODS AND EVILS*, TRANS. H. RACKHAM

Is intellectual life in these novels ever more than street fighting or empty pretension? It is ultimately through her friend Lila that both Lenù and the reader see an alternative perspective, a deeper value to the work of the mind. Early on, Lila might seem to be cut from the same competitive, status-driven cloth as Lenù. After dropping out of school, she becomes preoccupied with making money as a route out of poverty. She turns to making shoes, hoping by selling them to make herself and her family safe. Her shoemaking enterprise is taken over by her father, brother, and various suitors and deal makers; Lila turns to making herself beautiful, so that she can marry the successful grocer Stefano Carracci, leave poverty, and evade the clutches of her suitor, mafia thug Marcello Solara. Her new mode of successful competition is ruthlessly criticized by their school-teacher, Maestra Oliviero: "The beauty of mind that Cerullo had from childhood didn't find an outlet, Greco, and it has all ended up in her face, in her breasts, in her thighs, in her ass, places where it soon fades and it will be as if she had never had it."[42] All this suggests that for Lila and Lenù, school and intellectual life are simply ways out of poverty, humiliation, and powerlessness, a way that could be found alternately by success in business or marriage.

But the picture of Lila as a merely competitive striver, using whatever means necessary to advance herself, proves itself to be

superficial. On the contrary, Lila, for Lenù, is a source of spontaneous energy and interest: she animates otherwise dead
words and activities, she lives in an authentic reality that eludes
the other characters. Lenù feels that she is sometimes able to
share in Lila's spontaneous creative and intellectual activity. At
the opening of the first novel, *My Brilliant Friend*, she and Lila
buy a copy of *Little Women*:

> As soon as we were owners of the book we began to meet in
> the courtyard to read it, either silently, one next to the other,
> or aloud. We read it for months, so many times that the book
> became tattered and sweat-stained, it lost its spine, came un-
> threaded, sections fell apart. But it was our book, we loved it
> dearly.[43]

The little intellectual community formed by the girls over *Little
Women* is an island of contemplative passion in a life, in Lenù's
case, of impressing people and stringing together words. She believes that it has its source in Lila, and that she has no access to
it on her own.

Lenù and Lila read and study together, but they also reflect
on their community. They are preoccupied with the murder of
the neighborhood villain, Don Achille, and ponder whether the
neighborhood might be healed by a marriage between the son of
the victim and the daughter of the accused murderer: "We discussed it. We were twelve years old, but we walked among the
hot streets of the neighborhood, amid the dust and flies that occasional trucks stirred up as they passed, like two old ladies taking the measure of lives of disappointment."[44] Lenù describes
this imaginative discussion of the conflict within the community
as a "game," a way of reinventing their surroundings to make
them bearable. It is a godlike activity, an attempt at re-creation or
redemption.

Lila's spontaneous intellect has its most luminous symbol in her personal notebooks. Her notebooks contain, on Lenù's account, descriptions of trees and leaves, tools and their parts, buildings, and, "above all, colors," words, and ideas, along with narrative accounts of events in her life up to that point.[45] When Lila gives the notebooks to Lenù for safekeeping, she consumes them, first reading them to the point of memorizing them and then destroying them by throwing them into a river. The notebooks are the polar opposite of the empty political talk that enchants Lenù. Their contents are useless on their own, merely thoughtful and contemplative; their uselessness is compounded by their destruction and loss. They consist of thinking that goes nowhere and yet infects Lenù with its beauty and spontaneity.

The idea that Lila's special appeal lies in her existing for her own sake, in her holy uselessness, emerges much later, toward the end of the quartet of novels. Lenù reflects on what was especially attractive about Lila to Nino, the figure in the novel who most clearly represents the purely professional, striving intellectual. Lenù realizes that Nino's love interests have each gained him something in his career—apart from his love for Lila, which at the time caused him only grief and social setbacks. This enables her to articulate Lila's meaning for others:

> [Lila] possessed intelligence and didn't put it to use, but, rather, wasted it, like a great lady for whom all the riches of the world are merely a sign of vulgarity. That was the fact that must have beguiled Nino: the gratuitousness of Lila's intelligence. *She stood out among so many because she, naturally, did not submit to any training, to any use, or to any purpose.* All of us had submitted and that submission had—through trials,

failures, successes—reduced us. Only Lila, nothing and no one seemed to reduce her.[46]

This image of Lila as existing most for her own sake, especially as revealed in her use of her intelligence, appears again in the final pages of the quartet when we see her wandering the streets of Naples and writing a vast book on the city and its history that no one will ever read. All of Lila's own writings disappear: her diaries are dropped into the river by Lenù, she herself burns her childhood novel *The Blue Fairy* in a furnace, and her final work on Naples disappears when she does. In contrast, every book of Lenù's advances her, redounds to her credit or her discredit, brings her into the public eye.

The authentic exercise of the love of learning thus has a dark side in the novels. Lila reaches out for beauty and understanding and seeks to express herself in words and images. She is an artist, even a great artist, whose works are never seen or read; and something ought to strike us as strange about that. Her art is pure of social uses, to be sure—its destruction without use ensures that—but this type of purity seems infertile, trapped within one person.

Lila's concern that her work not be made public is the opposite of Lenù's constant use of the public outlet, her total focus on making an impression on others. But this dissimilarity reminds us that the two women have other opposite impulses: Lenù's experience of sexual pleasure against Lila's lack; Lenù's enjoyment of childbirth against Lila's resistance and fear. To produce art, by long tradition, is a sort of birth, a kind of fertility, a seeking after immortality. For all Lenù's empty status-consciousness, she is capable of this essential aspect of art where Lila is not. It is as if art requires spontaneous contemplative fire like Lila's as well as Lenù's social ambition, her wish to be seen.

The thought that art might require social ambition as well as pure contemplation ought to lead us to take a second look at Lenù's character. Of course, it is from Lenù the narrator that we have learned how status driven she is, as she compares herself with Lila the true, authentic intellectual. Her narration is not reliable: she denigrates herself and idealizes Lila. We can't be sure, in fact, that the useless, hidden, for-her-own-sake Lila really exists, or if she is Elena's fantasy, generated by her own self-hatred.

Lenù has moved from one world to another, from a poverty-stricken neighborhood riven by violence to a comfortable middle-class world where words are more common than blows. She is therefore haunted by the thought that she is always faking it, that others are doing it for real. Academics call this the "imposter syndrome"—it is the special disease of young graduate students, who arrive at their programs convinced that everyone else knows what they are talking about, and only they are steeped in ignorance, faking it at every step. It is not inauthenticity so much as the inner fear of inauthenticity, the awareness that one is not yet a part of the social class one is striving to join.

One sign that Lenù has exaggerated her own outward focus and status-consciousness is that she describes herself reading novels on her own, without talking to anyone about them or achieving any end result from them.[47] Likewise, her first novel emerges spontaneously. No one tells her to write it; she is imitating no one whom we see in the novel, except Lila with her diaries and her childhood work *The Blue Fairy*. Lenù's novel is evidently a reflection on her life; we know about it only that it contains a version of the story of her loss of virginity. She writes it in twenty days, and says that afterward the shame—the shame of being told to become a schoolteacher rather than a professor—passes out of her and into the book.[48] That the book emerges as a response to a humiliating diminution of her talent and status indicates that it springs from Lenù's ultimately competitive spirit. But its spontaneity, its coming forth on her terms, suggests that she has moved past merely passive responses to the prompts of her superiors, and that she means to carve out a place for herself that her masters have not imagined.

It is through Lenù, not Lila, that we get the novels' clearest picture of what art is and why it matters. Its purpose is to reflect on human life and find meaning in it: to "construct living hearts." Early in the third novel, Lenù describes what writing novels means to her after seeing her own first novel on the shelves of a bookstore:

> I knew what great literature was, I had done a lot of work in the classics, and it never occurred to me, while I was writing, that I was making something of value. But the effort of finding a form had absorbed me. And the absorption had become *that* book, an object that contained me. Now *I* was there, *exposed*, and seeing myself caused a violent pounding in my chest. I felt that not only in my book but in novels in general there was something that truly agitated me, a bare and throbbing heart, the same that had burst out of my chest in that distant moment when Lila had proposed that we write a story together. It had fallen to me to do it seriously. But was that what I wanted? To write, to write with purpose, to write better than I had already? And to study the stories of the past and the present to understand how they worked, and *to learn, learn everything about the world with the sole purpose of constructing living hearts*, which no one would ever do better than me, not even Lila if she had the opportunity?[49]

Here Elena's purpose in literature is laid out: in part, it is to construct a "living heart," a "bare and throbbing heart"—which turns out to be her own heart, herself contained in the book. It requires learning "everything about the world"; it is the contemplative activity that she and Lila undertake as children, talking like old women about the people they know in their neighborhood and striving to find the truth about them. And competition has a central role in this contemplative activity: the declaration that "no one would ever do better than me" echoes Lila's charge before her wedding that Lenù must be "best of everyone, boys and girls."[50]

What kind of intellectual activity is it to write one's own life, to draw a "beating heart"? It is the collection of fragments of experience into lines of narrative. It is an account of what a person loves, her desires, hopes, and ambitions, the springs of her actions. In the passage, Lenù describes it as her own heart, but surely she tries, in the four novels she is narrating, also to describe Lila's heart, and to capture in some way their love for each other.

The drawing of a beating heart is also, most clearly, the drawing of a living heart, a way of rescuing what is alive and concrete from dissolution and death. It is a way of seeking out a deathless truth. The universe of the Neapolitan novels is empty and chaotic; the starry sky, on Lila's account, is "only random shards of glass in a blue pitch."[51] As a teenager Lila responds with anger to a theological discourse that Lenù has generated for school:

You still waste time with these things, Lenù? We are flying over a ball of fire. The part that has cooled floats on the lava. On that part we construct the buildings, the bridges, and the streets, and every so often the lava comes out of Vesuvius or causes an earthquake that destroys everything. There are microbes everywhere that make us sick and die. There are wars. There is a poverty that makes us all cruel. Every second something might happen that will cause you such suffering that you'll never have enough tears.[52]

Lila's materialistic vision of a violent world that indifferently causes great suffering is never countered by any opposing vision in the book. The religion that lies behind Lenù's youthful theologizing is almost entirely absent from the lives of the characters, appearing only as another vehicle of achievement (as here) or another instrument of control (as when Lenù's mother protests her not being married in a church). Against the indifferent violence of the world there stands only the work of literature, the capturing of living human beings in action, the reflection on what makes them move, thrive, and suffer. This reflection is undertaken not alone but in friendship, in mutual support and mutual fascination, in the pursuit of self-knowledge with another. The work of art is collaborative.

Thoughtful readers of the Neapolitan novels may disagree as to whether Elena transcends her status-driven ambition in the end, creating a real work of art that exists for its own sake; or whether she truly loves Lila or means only to ingest her, to use her. I think that she succeeds on both counts in overcoming her worst elements. If so, we can see ambition as a part—but only a part—of a creative drive, as fuel for real contemplative work that is shared with others, as an engine of real art. But that is not to ignore the ways in which it entraps characters like Elena or Nino in delusions about themselves or about the world. In the universe of the book, it takes a real love for another human being, a true friendship, to override the destructive forces of ambition and so provide the only comfort and redemption available in it.

———

Augustine overcomes his false love of learning, ambition upheld by the love of spectacle, thanks to a discipline of reading and a hunger for the truth. He is haunted by an impulse that he gradually learns to articulate: that truth ought to organize his life, that it is his highest end and the condition for his flourishing. Elena Greco fuses her competitive ambition, her desire to show others what she is made of, her desire to see and be seen, with a contemplative friendship, an admiration for the beauty of learning that lies beyond use. So we have examined two ways in which the love of learning might overcome typical abuses of the intellect: ambition, self-deception, or ways of using the mind to create soothing or exciting spectacles. The love of learning has emerged as something profoundly serious, something that can change a life, a source of our highest aspirations—to know, to love, to flourish in our full humanity.

CHAPTER 3

The Uses of Uselessness

Of all men, those alone are at leisure who take time for wisdom, they alone live; for they are not content to be good guardians of their own lifetime only. They annex every age to their own; all the years that have gone before them are an addition to their store. Unless we are most ungrateful, all those men, glorious fashioners of holy thoughts, were born for us; for us they have prepared a way of life. By other men's labors we are led to the sight of things most beautiful that have been wrested from darkness and brought into the light; from no age are we shut out, we are admitted to all ages, and if it is our wish, by greatness of soul, to pass beyond the narrow limits of human weakness, there is a great stretch of time through which we may roam. We may argue with Socrates, we may doubt with Carneades, find peace with Epicurus, overcome human nature with the Stoics, exceed it with the Cynics. Since the nature of things allows us to enter into fellowship with every age, why should we not turn from this paltry and fleeting span of time and surrender ourselves with all our soul to the past, which is boundless, which is eternal, which we share with our betters?

—SENECA, *ON THE SHORTNESS OF LIFE*,
TRANS. J. W. BASORE, MODIFIED

The Temptation of the Active Life

I have tried to describe the corruption of learning by the love of money and by the desire for social success. The most difficult case I have saved for last: the corruption of learning by politics and political goals. The source of the difficulty is that politics meets learning in two very distinct ways, but they often become entangled with each other. When the life of the mind is directed toward money and status, intellectual institutions tend to establish or maintain social hierarchies, or what are fashionably called structures of power. It is natural to judge that these same practices and institutions ought to be used to undo or reshape these hierarchies, to counteract forces of injustice or exclusion within them. So we find the first way that politics meets intellectual life: as an attempt to remedy its corruption and to recover some of its general human character. However, the impact of the dedication of intellectual life to social justice is perverse.

When we attempt to produce just outcomes from the top down, we shortcut the communion of the reader with the author and so suppress the egalitarian community of learning that, for instance, W.E.B. Du Bois found through reading and study. Worse, the longing for justice is reduced to a set of rules for the use of language or for which opinions can be expressed. The correct justice-promoting words become tools for gatekeepers, protecting a hierarchy in the end not obviously different from the one that prompted the revolution. Social justice becomes not only trivialized, but also emptied of content, used for purposes counter to its professed aims.

And yet, to react too sharply against the politicization of academic life can cover over something crucial. As a graduate student in philosophy, I was haunted by the prospect of uselessness. The suffering world cries out to be fixed. How can we choose intellectual life over a life of action? How can we spare time to contemplate, if that means lost lives and livelihoods through inactivity? Even more, how could we justify the work of the mind as central to our life, rather than being simply one diverting hobby among others?

As intellectual life in our common culture becomes mixed with the love of money and with social ambition, it is also mixed with politics, and thus the difference between the contemplative life and the life of action or the life of political service becomes blurred. The learning for its own sake that formed a key part of anglophone intellectual culture in the twentieth century, which shaped and expressed its egalitarian ideals, has gradually been traded for learning for social utility, for the sake of "making a difference."

Our communities could not function without work for justice and for the material forms of well-being, which make possible all of the higher goods in human life, leisure, study, art, and community. No one lives a life without any practical tasks, and some will find their lives more satisfying if the leisure of intellectual life is taken in snatches, in breaks, in short periods, as they wind down at the end of the day. Likewise, some professional training may be necessary for some forms of practical work for the community. It therefore has some place at institutions that provide training in the professions. But its conquest of the whole enterprise of higher education, and the degradation of intellectual life in general that results from such conquest, must be resisted.

Yet, the vision of the suffering world that shook me from my comfortable flourishing as a graduate student, a vision experienced by many at one time or another, is revelatory. It uncovers all sorts of comfortable falsehoods and pointless tasks. It turns books to straw and reduces the pay of prestigious positions to guilt and ennui. So it should. Our work ought to serve real human needs. But there is a difference between service and corrosive forms of activism, however difficult it may be to articulate and to find in practice. Identifying ways that the desire to make a difference may be caught up in structures of social distinction or in self-regarding spectacles will be a good place to start.

Ferrante on Politics and Ambition

Our concerns for social goods face certain dangers. Like the desire to learn or the desire for basic comforts, they can get distorted and emptied of value when our sources of motivation are disordered. Lenù and Lila from the Neapolitan novels, once again, provide key examples.

Talking about politics is useless in the Neapolitan novels—or rather, its use is primarily for social advancement. Here most of the talk about politics is presented as exchanges of empty words disconnected from the lives of the suffering characters, as speeches utterly without efficacy beyond social advancement and social exclusion. That, at any rate, is the role they play in the life of Lenù, the academically and socially ambitious girl who seeks a way out of the diminishments of her poor neighborhood. Lenù's mentor in high school is her teacher Professor Galiani, who gives her books about politics (never literature) and encourages her to read newspapers. During this time Lenù reads "out of duty" and stops by the grocery where Lila works to share her new knowledge:

> While I devoured [a sandwich], I would articulate, in good Italian, statements I had memorized from Professor Galiani's books and newspapers. I would mention, let's say, "the atrocious reality of the Nazi extermination camps," or "what men were able to do and what they can do today as well," or "the atomic threat and the obligation to peace," or the fact that "as a result of subduing the forces of nature with the tools that we

invent, we find ourselves today at the point where the force of our tools has become a greater concern than the forces of nature," or "the need for a culture that combats and eliminates suffering," or the idea that "religion will disappear from men's consciousness when, finally, we have constructed a world of equals, without class distinctions, and with a sound scientific conception of society and life."[1]

Lenù memorizes words and phrases in order to ingratiate herself with her teacher and to show her superiority to her old friend (while incongruously chomping on a sandwich). Lenù's ultimate cruelty to Lila in this regard is shown when she brings her to a party at Professor Galiani's house and, once there, ignores her as an insignificant housewife. The friend with whom she has shared intellectual interests since childhood is discarded as socially useless or embarrassing.

Lila has intellectual interests of her own; it is for this reason that she wanted to attend the party, to see the world that her youthful marriage to a grocer has kept her from. She responds to Elena's insult with a brutal and accurate takedown of the gathering she has witnessed, as her husband, Stefano, picks them up from the party. She describes the elite partygoers to him:

> If you were up there, Sté, all you'd see is parrots going *cocorico, cocorico*. You couldn't understand a word they're saying and they didn't even understand each other. . . . You too, Lenù, look out or you'll be the parrot's parrot. . . . You and Sarratore's son [Nino], the same. *The world brigade for peace; we have the technical capability; hunger, war.* But do you really work that hard in school so you can say things just like he does? *Whoever finds a solution to the problems is working for peace.* Bravo. . . . You, too, you want to be a puppet from the neighborhood who performs so you can be welcomed into the home of those

people? You want to leave us alone in our own shit, cracking our skulls, while all of you go *cocorico cocorico*, hunger, war, working class, peace?[2]

It is partly bitterness that drives Lila to this outburst, anger at her humiliating exclusion from the social elite at the party. All the same, the novels bear out her diagnosis: intellectuals talk politics to advance themselves while the people they grew up with continue to live in poverty and violence.

Political talk builds an exterior wall of words, a set of opinions built and reinforced by competitive passions: "I am this sort of person and not that." It is a way to avoid the encounter with the difficult and humiliating social reality to which one belongs or for which one is responsible. Further on, I call this process "opinionization," by which I mean the reduction of thinking and perception to simple slogans or prefabricated positions, a reduction motivated by fear, competition, and laziness.

Lenù's ambition is successful. By learning to parrot important-sounding political words and opinions, eventually she wins over the middle-class family of Professor Airota at the conclusion of her studies at university, and marries the great professor's son Pietro. Her engagement and marriage to Pietro are instrumental in launching her career as a writer. When she first meets Pietro's family, she finds that they speak in terms similar to those used by Professor Galiani and her political friends at university. The father and his daughter have friendly arguments:

> Arguments like: you've been trapped by inter-class collaboration; you call it a trap, I call it mediation; mediation in which the Christian Democrats always and only win; the politics of the center left is difficult; if it's difficult, go back to being socialists; you're not reforming a thing; in our place what would you do; revolution and revolution and revolution; revolution

is taking Italy out of the Middle Ages, without us socialists in the government the students who talk about sex in school would be in jail and so would those who distribute pacifist leaflets; I want to see how you'd manage with the Atlantic pact; we were always against the war and against all imperialism; you govern with the Christian Democrats but will you stay anti-American?[3]

In Elena's narrative these random catchphrases have been strung into a sequence of a conversation; she describes the phrases as "infused with warmth." Still, in her description they are as colorless and empty as the words she previously parroted to Lila. She enters into the conversation with the Airota family by saying "hyperbolically, 'The Americans, after Hiroshima and Nagasaki, should be brought to trial for crimes against humanity.'" The family responds with approval, and she spits out more "words, scraps of phrases memorized at various times."[4] She has convinced them that she belongs.

To some extent the emptiness of Lenù's political interest, like the grade-driven intellectual activity we saw in her earlier, is a function of her youth. She is making her way into a new world, and must learn its ways and customs at first by rote. In this way she might be seen as resembling the characters we began with, Steve Martin or Martin Eden, who enter intellectual life in order to impress someone, and then find their way into something different and better. But the emptiness and inefficacy of political speech is a theme throughout the four novels, and endures into Lenù's maturity.

The overwhelming impression of political activity presented by the novels is that political words and what passes for political thinking are empty pretense, the ticket to social advancement for individuals. Political action moves without contact with reality, and is in fact motivated by a concerted attempt to avoid the difficulties for which it pretends concern. But there is one interesting exception: the journalistic exposés that Lenù and Lila undertake together of the brutality and corruption in their communities, first of Bruno Soccavi's brutal sausage factory and later of the criminal Solara family. These are attempts to use words to uncover truth and so to shame the violence out of Naples.

But although the journalistic writings reflect reality in crucial ways, they have no positive impact; they do not persuade or influence. Rather, both exposés inspire violence and murder: between the Left and the Right around Bruno's factory in *Those Who Leave and Those Who Stay*, and against Lila in *The Story of the Lost Child*. The idea that words can overcome violence and improve real conditions turns out to be a fantasy; the image of the school competition that spills over into throwing rocks in the streets is ultimately the truer one. The promise of the public exposure of wrongdoing, of reflecting real life in public in the hope of effecting change, is never realized. Political words are scramblings for power—and the true, well-intentioned political words contrived collaboratively by Elena and Lila are no exception.

The Quixotic Love of Justice

The division of political concern into the superficial and the fruitless that we find in the Neapolitan novels may seem too severe. Surely if we seek justice in earnest, not to advance socially but rather to humble ourselves, to understand and serve our neighbor, our search will be both deep and worthwhile.

In Simone Petrement's biography of philosopher Simone Weil, we see Weil at first intensely involved in the political interests of university students in Paris in the 1930s. Weil writes essay after essay siding with one faction and against another. The unions and the parties divide themselves into ever smaller and angrier fragments, divided by acronyms and alphabet soups as much as by principle. Weil conceives a desire for the real thing: to be poor among the poor. She takes leave from her job teaching philosophy and spends a year working in factories. Weak and sickly, she is fired more than once for not meeting work quotas. Her writing takes on a tone of awe and humility. Her interest in Christianity, according to Petrement, takes hold of her at this time.

Reading Petrement's account of this sickly philosophy teacher trying to work an assembly line provokes both admiration and pity. Petrement relates one story of Weil traveling in the countryside and persuading a passing farmer to let her drive his plough. She overturns it and reduces the farmer to wrath.[5] At this moment, I think, the reader sees that Weil is a Don Quixote, enchanted by fantasies and haunted by the hope of authenticity, unable to accept her given social reality as a middle-class teacher and as a person of poor health and limited hand-eye coordination. We see grandiosity as well in her attempt to join the fight of the Spanish loyalists against Franco, only to be forced to leave the country to get medical treatment: this is a woman who does not know what she is.

And yet Weil's desire is deeply admirable—she recognizes the phoniness of the Paris leftists and wants the wisdom of real poverty and manual labor. She knows that communion and solidarity are not effected by concerned statements, but by shared activity. At one point, Weil asks to live and work with the farming parents of a pupil at her school, the Bellevilles. Her inability to work well and her speeches drive the Bellevilles to distraction. Mme. Belleville wrote about her:

> My husband and I used to say: the poor young girl, so much study has driven her out of her wits; and we were sorry for her;

while really it was we who were out of our depth. But what could we do? All the intellectuals we knew put barriers between themselves and the peasants. Simone Weil threw down those barriers and put herself on our level.[6]

Belleville captures both the Quixotic humor—Weil is out of her wits—and the nobility of the young woman's behavior. Weil is trapped in an intellectual world in which she flourishes, but which is disconnected from the suffering of its surrounding community. Humiliation is the price of connection. Otherwise, her only power is in words, and words disconnect from deeds as sparks fly upward.

Something in us loves the spectacle of our own action, and reduces our best impulses to narcissistic fantasy. So pervasive and profound is this feature of human nature that it can seem inescapable. Weil reminds us of John L. Sullivan, the filmmaker protagonist of Preston Sturges's 1941 film *Sullivan's Travels*.[7] Sturges's film hides in its screwball comedy a profound meditation on the ways in which an earnest desire to do good can go wrong.

Sullivan has made his fortune writing popular comedies. Nonetheless, in an era of depression and war, he is haunted by the failure of his work to address the suffering of the poor and marginalized. He aspires to produce a weighty film allegorizing the struggle between labor and capital. Mocked for his new seriousness and his privileged background by his circle of advisers, he decides he must experience real poverty for himself. He plans to ride the freights and commune with the impoverished common man for a time, to see for himself firsthand what poverty is really like.

Sullivan's attempts to experience poverty are a colossal failure. His handlers insist on following him in a huge vehicle with a fully stocked kitchen, complete with chef, as well as a doctor and press team. He gets rid of them and hitches a long ride on a truck. He emerges to find himself back in Hollywood, and he is joined there by a love interest played by Veronica Lake. The would-be hobos hop a freight that brings them, hungry and out of cash, to the Las Vegas diner where Sullivan's handlers happen to be waiting for him. After a brief, final pampering, he and Lake are able to shake their support staff (apart from a discreet cameraman) and launch their enterprise in earnest. The narrative gives way to a montage of their experiences of jungle camps, shelters infested with pests, inedible meals at soup kitchens, and demeaning pickup work. The images are poignant, thanks to the surroundings, but convey a quite enjoyable adventure. Sullivan's social concern culminates in the picturesque. When the pair are reduced to eating out of a genuine trash can, they give up and head back to normal life.

By calling attention to Sullivan's voyeuristic perspective, the film's images of the poor and the desperate reach the viewer with greater effect. Sullivan himself is haunted by the failure of his efforts to become poor. After the second "rescue" by his handlers, he complains, "It's funny the way everything keeps shoving me back to Hollywood . . . as if some force were saying 'Get back where you belong. . . . You don't belong to real life, you phony you.'"

Sturges thus honors the movement of the heart toward the poor and the marginalized. Yet he diagnoses its inefficacy with brutal comic accuracy. An impassible gulf lies between the poor and the socially concerned middle and upper classes. Concern without knowledge or experience reeks of self-serving condescension. But to experience poverty as one among many possible learning experiences is not to experience poverty at all. In the face of this gulf, concern for the poor quickly collapses under the narcissism of the narrative, and self-regard wins an easy victory over self-sacrifice. Sullivan's press team is on hand to translate his experiences into attractive catchphrases. The desire to make a difference turns out to be a desire to make a splash.

Sullivan says farewell to his adventure with the poor by handing out cash in a final media event. Here the tone of the film shifts dramatically from light to dark, as he meets real poverty for the first time. He is knocked out cold, robbed of his cash and his boots, and thrown into a freight car. The perpetrator is hit by a train and the boots indicate to the police that it is Sullivan who was killed. Sullivan himself emerges from his freight car and gets into a fight with a railroad bull while still disoriented. His protestations of his true identity are ignored as ravings, and he is sentenced to six years hard labor.

In the fearsome rural prison to which he is sentenced, Sullivan finds out what it means to be poor, helpless, and subject to the arbitrary whims of coercive authority. While in earlier ventures into poverty his upper-class background made him ludicrous, here it manifests as a failure to know his place that provokes violent and cruel reprisals from the warden. A local church invites the prisoners to a viewing of slapstick cartoons. Amid the roars of laughter of his fellow inmates, Sullivan comes to understand the value of his previous work. Once a final plot twist returns him to his former state of comfort and affluence, he renounces his attempts at more serious filmmaking. He concludes, "There's a lot to be said for making people laugh. Don't you know that's all some people have? It's not much, but it's better than nothing in this cockeyed caravan."

It is natural to be repulsed by the resolution of the film. Sullivan uses his social status to pry himself from prison and returns to Hollywood luxury, supporting his swimming-pool lifestyle by providing sources of laughter to the desperate and impoverished. All the same, Sullivan's final insight is real. He

understands that his ordinary work all on its own meets a crucial human need. He has overcome the love of spectacle, and
found the value of loving service.

Thanks to his lucky and luckily brief escape from the trap of
phoniness into real suffering, Sullivan finds that comedy is one
of the little human things, totally useless and yet completely
essential for anything we would recognize as human flourishing. As Sullivan sees his fellow prisoners dissolve in laughter, he
sees that a little splinter of the human good can find its way even
into the darkest places—places where the little human things may
be the only human things at all.

The difference between the little human things and their cultivated counterparts should not be exaggerated. There are ten
million reasons for pursuing comedy, art, music, and intellectual
life to the highest available level of excellence. But achievement
doesn't justify the practice: the human need does. Music is pointless in a world in which no one recognizes the value of ordinary
piano lessons or singing in harmony, even if highly trained mu-
sicians continue to perform the finest art music. Likewise, there's
no point in getting to the bottom of Plato's dialogues if human
beings do not shoot the bull at the lake or mull over the justice
of things while washing windows. The little human things make
the human needs manifest; without those needs in mind, the
grander endeavors lose their way.

Work—real work, work that matters—serves others by providing for a human need, some piece of the human good. For
most of us, including the poor, serving others through work is
the most obvious way that we "transform lives for the benefit of
society." Garbage collectors don't "make a difference" in the sense
that today's young people are constantly encouraged to do. They
will never be featured on a major media platform for their inno-
vative contribution to society. But most of us are far removed

from what it means to live in a filthy street and can hardly imagine what it would mean to rely on individual initiative to remove household waste. Collecting garbage is a form of service, just as producing comedy is. That comparison should begin to suggest to us just how superficial and how hostile to the interests of humanity our notion of "making a difference" really is.

Living Out of Books

This very talk may obscure everything we know nothing of now, and who knows but that silence may lead us to it.
—DOROTHY DAY, *FROM UNION SQUARE TO ROME*

How can intellectual life help us to serve others? Let's return to the thought that the value of intellectual life lies in its broadening and deepening of our humanity. As it turns out, the humanizing effect of learning does not seem to depend on routes of inquiry or on authors who seek the human universal at the expense of the factional. It begins in the readers' or the inquirers' deep engagement with learning, their assumption of the responsibility of being transformed by what they learn, their treatment of learning as a part of getting down into the depths of life. In other words, a reader or thinker driven by the desire for the weightier and the better—what I have called the virtue of seriousness—will find the human core even in books with a partial view. It is the virtue of seriousness that permits our thinking and learning to shape our moral lives and our lives with others. Without it, intellectual life risks superficiality, conformity, and complicity with evil.

I lack an argument that the virtue of seriousness is sufficient to shape one's thinking toward ways of serving others, but I do have an example: Dorothy Day, the American Catholic convert

and cofounder with Peter Maurin of the Catholic Worker movement. Day on her own account learned to love humanity and
live accordingly through serious reading and the constant attempt to live what she read.[8]

Day was raised in a middle-class family in Chicago. Through
an intense intellectual life consisting of broad reading and reflection, she underwent first a conversion to socialism, and some
years later a conversion to Catholicism. The Catholic spiritual-
ity that she lived rested on voluntary poverty: the communities
that she founded practice hospitality to all, house many home-
less, and survive largely on donations. Day strove to minimize to
the greatest extent possible any practical difference between the
poor guests at the "houses of hospitality" and their middle-class
volunteers. So too she practiced a form of prophecy: she spoke
against the atom bomb on principle and refused to cooperate
with the civil defense drills of the 1950s, drills designed to inure
the public to the use of nuclear weapons. Despite its blinding
moral truth, the case against atomic and nuclear weapons has
never had any political bite, so the efforts were without political
impact; they were a form of Christian witness for its own sake.

Day told her biographer Robert Coles that she wanted to be
remembered for two things: her conversations with her guests,
whom she called her "teachers," and her love of books:

> Another thing—I'd like people to say that "she really did love
> those books!" I'm always telling people to read Dickens or
> Tolstoi, or read Orwell, or read Silone. I could be one of your
> teachers—though I'm not a great one for analyzing those nov-
> els; I want to *live* by them! That's the "meaning of my life"
> [she quotes the question asked by a student]—to live up to
> the moral vision of the Church, and of some of my favorite
> writers.[9]

It is a strange claim for a lifelong activist to make, that the meaning of her life consisted somehow in her love of books. What
could she mean?

Her two autobiographies describe her constant reading from
childhood: "It was never one book that engrossed me but a
dozen. I was hungry for knowledge and had to devour volumes."[10]
She was transformed especially by two socialist novelists of the
early twentieth century, Upton Sinclair and Jack London; and
throughout her writings she mentions Tolstoy, Dostoyevsky, and
Dickens, three novelists who wrote with an intense awareness
of the poor. In her first autobiography she recalled the effect on
her of these novels:

> When what I read was particularly class-conscious, I used to
> turn from the park with all its beauty and peacefulness and
> walk down to North Avenue and over West through slum dis-
> tricts, and watch the slatternly women and unkempt children
> and ponder over the poverty of the homes as contrasted with
> the wealth along the shore drive. I wanted even then to play
> my part. I wanted to write such books that thousands upon
> thousands of readers would be convinced of the injustice of
> things as they were.[11]

There is an almost unearthly directness to the interaction with
books that Day describes here. She reads about something and
walks out to look at it. Over time, the books open up reality to
her, through the medium of words and authors. It is for this reason, I think, that she refers to the books as "companions" and
compares her life with books to her life with the living human
beings who lived in her houses.

And yet her reading could have gone in any number of direc-
tions. A reader of Sinclair, London, or Dickens could take refuge in empty, self-aggrandizing talk about the injustice of things.

Such talk would find a hospitable audience among the liberal middle class of New York or Chicago, as Day knows well. Or the books could have remained distractions, idle forms of entertainment.

Day is a writer committed to encouragement, unwilling to speak ill of anyone, even her preconverted self. Yet in her autobiography *From Union Square to Rome*, Day describes using reading to escape from a feeling of profound depression, in which she is "overwhelmed by the terror and the blackness of both life and death":

> During the evening I read desperately, trying to rescue myself from the wall of silence which seemed to close me in.
>
> But this makes me realize that often talk is an escape from doing anything. We chatter on and on to cover our feelings and to hide from ourselves and others our own futility.
>
> Of course conversation is often spirited and uplifts me as some books do. It helps me to glimpse the meaning in things and jolts me out of the rut in which I have been ambling along. I am spurred on to the pursuit of knowledge by a renewed love of knowledge. And yet the trouble with these conversations is that often they are not spontaneous. Some of my liberal friends, for instance, have gatherings, Sunday afternoons or Thursday nights, and the little crowd which comes feels itself a group and the conversation often seems pompous and self-congratulatory.
>
> This exaltation of the articulate obscures the fact that there are millions of people in this world who feel and in some way carry on courageously even though they cannot talk or reason brilliantly. This very talk may obscure everything we know nothing of now, and who knows but that silence may lead us to it.[12]

A sense of her own emptiness drives her to read for the sake of distraction, a drive she compares to the self-congratulatory conversation she sometimes enjoys with her liberal friends. She judges it unwise to shield or obscure feelings of sorrow, inferiority, and "futility," suggesting that it is better to face them bravely, as even ordinary, inarticulate people are able to do.

Saint John of the Cross describes the human capacities to re-member, understand, and will as "deep caverns of sense"—infinitely deep caves that can be filled only by God. But, he says, the presence of the least "creature affection" in them, the least attachment to a matter of sense, makes awareness of their emp-tiness impossible. So human beings with any attachment will not long for what can fill them: "for in this life any trifle that remains within them suffices to keep them so cumbered and fascinated that they are neither conscious of their loss nor do they miss the immense blessings that might be theirs, so that they cannot re-ceive these blessings that might be theirs, nor are they aware of their own capacity."[13] Saint John indicates that it is extremely painful to perceive the emptiness of one's mind, the bottomless indeterminacy in one's capacity to receive, remember, and un-derstand. The incentive to fill oneself with "trifles" is obvious. He argues on the contrary that the magnitude of the pain of inner emptiness measures the joy we are capable of when filled by God.

Just as Day's upward movement, spurred by the love of learn-ing, risks collapsing into smug superiority, so too her downward movement into poverty risks a sort of thrill seeking. When we ask what Day sees as drawing her on from childhood to activism to the Catholic Church, it is not a stretch to see a longing for communion with others, especially the poor. But she is con-cerned that it is mixed with baser motives:

Was this desire to be with the poor and the mean and abandoned not unmixed with a distorted desire to be with the dis-
sipated? Mauriac tells of a subtle pride and hypocrisy: "There
is a kind of hypocrisy which is worse than that of the Phari-
sees; it is to hide behind Christ's example in order to follow
one's own lustful desires and to seek out the company of the
dissolute."[14]

Day calls this desire elsewhere "prideful humility," and she seems
to mean primarily the desire to escape conventional prohibitions
against sex or drugs. But I wonder whether another danger is also
on her mind in her concern with thrill seeking among the poor.
Thrill seeking—what I have called the love of spectacle—is
found in the more lurid passages of Sinclair or London. Is it only
for love of the poor that we seek the knowledge that working
people are regularly lost in the sausage machines, or that a young
boy in the stockyards of Chicago can be killed and eaten by rats,
as Sinclair describes in *The Jungle*? These stories may reflect reality, yet may attract us more out of fascination with their details
than out of love of humanity. We may visit prisoners out of com-
passion for them, but we may also thrill at the drama, the clang
of the bars, the foul smell from the cafeteria. Day does not dwell
on these darker parts of a human soul, but she knows they are
there. Why else is she egged on to greater authenticity, greater
identification between herself and the poor she served? Why is
a second conversion necessary?

On Day's account her Catholic conversion, like her socialist
conversion, is partly effected through books. Among the books
that haunt her life even before her turn to Catholicism is the
Bible, especially the Psalms. She writes of reading a Bible during
her first time in jail for a suffragist protest: "How could anyone
who has known human sorrow and human joy fail to respond

to these words? *Out of the depths I have cried to thee, O Lord . . ."*
It is the *humanity* of the Psalms that strikes her—their human
joy and sorrow. In this telling, the words on the page strike her
in just the same way as the other human beings in jail strike her.
Not only does the Psalm display the humanity of the people of
the past; it reaches into the here and now. She goes on to explain
how the words of the Psalm connected her with her fellow
inmates:

> All through those weary first days in jail when I was in soli-
> tary confinement, the only thoughts that brought comfort
> to my soul were those lines in the Psalms that expressed the
> terror and misery of man suddenly stricken and aban-
> doned. Solitude and hunger and weariness of spirit—these
> sharpened my perceptions so that I suffered not only my
> own sorrow but the sorrows of those about me. I was no
> longer myself. I was man. I was no longer a young girl, part
> of a radical movement seeking justice for those oppressed, I
> was the oppressed. I was that drug addict, screaming and
> tossing in her cell, beating her head against the wall. I was
> that shoplifter who for rebellion was sentenced to solitary.
> I was that woman who had killed her children, who had
> murdered her lover.
>
> The blackness of hell was all about me. The sorrows of the
> world encompassed me. I was like one gone down into the pit.
> Hope had forsaken me. I was that mother whose child had
> been raped and slain. I was the mother who had borne the
> monster who had done it. I was even that monster, feeling in
> my own heart every abomination.[15]

Her suffering in solitary confinement and the words of the Psalm
open up to Day a participation in what is broadly human, the
shared lot of human beings. She identifies with other inmates,

sharing their miseries. Paradoxically, the sense of union that she finds with others is found in solitude, without direct communication with anyone.

Day's accustomed writing style is a cool and matter-of-fact humility; the emotional drama shown here is rare. Accordingly, just after this passage she apologizes for its heightened emotion and even apparent exaggeration. She explains that most people protect themselves from the sufferings of others, and that by "accepting hardship and poverty as the way in life in which to walk" she has made herself susceptible to those sufferings.[16] I suspect that Day breaks her accustomed tone here because she is disclosing an essential piece of her inner life. She reveals her sense of unity with the suffering heart of the human race, and how that unity is mediated by words, by books, as well as by the lived reality that the books goaded her to seek out.

The Psalms continue to haunt Day somewhat later, when she is working as a nurse and still an atheist, although occasionally attending church services: "One day I told myself as I knelt there, I would have to stop and think, to question my own position: 'What is man, that Thou art mindful of him, O Lord?' What were we here for, what were we doing, what was the meaning of our lives?"[17] Here Day is not only feeling, but thinking and questioning. The Psalm has asked a universal question, a human question, which Day understands as one that must be taken to heart in real life. Again, her thinking and questioning might have taken alternative routes: she might have wondered what the Hebrew word for "mindful" is, or how the Psalms functioned in ancient Jewish liturgical practice. These inquiries might have produced a satisfying feeling of knowing, but they would not be quite serious, certainly not as serious as the changing shape of her life.

Once Day's search for the human and the general, as mediated through books, is noticed, it becomes obvious that her autobiographical writing overflows with similar passages:

> For a long time now, I had thought I could not have a child. A book I read years ago, in school, *Silas Marner*, expressed the sorrow of a mother bereft of her child, and it expressed, too, my sorrow at my childless state. Just a few months ago, I read it again, with a longing in my heart for a baby.[18]

Day frequently calls attention to her feelings and experiences as ordinary, as universal, as human. When she describes her work nursing during the First World War she points to the breadth of the experience: "straight nursing, which delights every woman's heart."[19] Or she will sum up her experiences in a general way, introducing the main narrative in her first autobiography: "After all, the experiences I have had are more or less universal. Suffering, sadness, repentance, love, we have all known these. They are easiest to bear when one remembers their universality, when we remember that we are all members or potential members of the Mystical Body of Christ."[20] Day here refers to the Catholic teaching that the members of the Church make up the Mystical Body of Christ. Each member shares in the suffering of the others while sharing the suffering of Christ himself, and thereby share in the ongoing redemptive act of Christ. She speaks in the autobiographies of the version of this teaching found on the radical Left into which she first converted. A second jail stay reminds her of the words of union leader Eugene Debs: "While there is a lower class, I am of it, and while there is a criminal element, I am of it, and while there is a soul in prison, I am not free."[21] The burning desire that apparently shapes Day's life is to live as deeply in the broad community of humanity as possible, to share the sufferings of anyone who suffers.

Day describes the continuity between her two conversions as stemming from the love of the poor, the love of humanity: "Because I sincerely loved His poor, He taught me to know Him. And when I think of the little I ever did, I am filled with hope and love for all those others devoted to the cause of social justice."[22] Her sympathy for human beings depicted in books has transferred into real people, not automatically—for, again, alternative paths were possible for her—but because of her hard thinking about her own life and the lives of others, thinking driven by her deepest desires. Her love of humanity has changed her vision of the world from one exclusively concerned with justice in the here and now to dependence on God and union with him.

Day's humanism draws her also to study William James. She makes it clear that it was James's *The Varieties of Religious Experience* more than the saccharine pious literature she encountered elsewhere that prepared her for her Catholic conversion.[23] Perhaps she resisted its heavy sweetness; or perhaps too the pious literature was narrow and factional, written in a sort of jargon that only insiders could understand.

James's work in *Varieties* consists in an earnest attempt to find what is generally human in the various kinds of religious experience.[24] He thus hopes to gather the moral fruits of religious devotion in an age in which he considers the belief in supernatural entities to be impossible. He carefully examines the experiences of believers and determines that the "eradication of self" that he considers to be central to morality requires no dramatic experience, and certainly no religious one. The features of religious experience, even asceticism and voluntary poverty, are general routes to human forms of excellence, and they can be developed in a godless age as well as in a religious one.

Just as Day moves past the factionalism of Sinclair or London to a broad, lived humanism, so too she reaches past James's atheistic humanism to a religious, Catholic humanism. In both cases, she is held and drawn on by the universal, the desire for communion with all human beings. James's humanistic approach enables her to see religion as a way of belonging to humanity rather than rising above it. Day is a free reader, one who does not evade the responsibility of reading or of learning, seeking after knowledge of human life and allowing herself to be changed by what she understands.

The Use of the Inner World

I have argued that intellectual life properly understood cultivates a space of retreat within a human being, a place where real reflection takes place. We step back from concerns of practical benefit, personal or public. We withdraw into small rooms, literal or internal. In the space of retreat we consider fundamental questions: what human happiness consists in, the origins and nature of the universe, whether human beings are part of nature, and whether and how a truly just community is possible. From the space of retreat emerges poetry, mathematics, and distilled wisdom articulated in words or manifested silently in action. The space of retreat is a place of escape: the prisoner, the working person, the beleaguered mother all find in the work of the intellect a dignity otherwise impinged on by their surroundings.

I earlier pointed to the beautiful examples showing the impact of grassroots intellectual movements that Jonathan Rose describes in *The Intellectual Life of the British Working Classes*. Rose's workers cultivate an inner world not subject to poverty's power to diminish: it is a source of insight and understanding, and a source of dignity denied by circumstances. So the

account of learning given by the cotton spinner Charles Camp-
bell (b. 1793):

> The lover of learning, however straitened his circumstances,
> or rugged his condition, has yet a source of enjoyment within
> himself that the world never dreams of. . . . Perhaps he is solv-
> ing a problem of Euclid, or soaring with Newton amidst the
> planetary world, and endeavouring to discover the nature and
> properties of that invisible attraction by which the Almighty
> mind has subjected inanimate matter to laws that resemble the
> operations of intelligence; or descending from the harmony
> of the spheres, he contemplates the principle of animal life,
> and explores the intricate labyrinths of physiological phenom-
> ena. . . . Pursuing the footsteps of Locke and Reid, he traces
> the origins of his own ideas, feeling, and passions: or . . . he
> unbends the wing of his imagination, and solaces his weary
> mind in the delightful gardens of the classic muse of poetry
> and music.[25]

Intellectual life provides an escape in that it is beyond "strait-
ened . . . circumstances," but that escape is again a flight into
realities beyond oneself: animal behavior, astronomy, and the
mechanics of the inner life. The intellect has no limit to its subject matter: it reaches greedily for the whole of everything. It was
the prospect of somehow holding the whole world within oneself that led Plato and Aristotle to think of the intellect as something divine, as offering the furthest heights to which a human
being could reach.

But my use of Rose's book to illustrate my own thesis about
the separation of intellectual life from politics is a bit dishon-
est, or at least ironic. Rose intends to show the social utility of
study and the work of the mind: the grassroots intellectual
movements that he chronicles were also movements of

political liberation. The striving for intellectual development for working people was part and parcel of the Labour movement in Britain and similar movements in the United States. And yet, it is impossible to read the testimonies themselves without seeing that intellectual life mattered to these people regardless of its political efficacy. Take Alice Foley, a socialist cotton-mill worker (b. 1891), writing of how her new intellectual life radicalized her:

> [A former croft worker] hated the industrial system and had found liberation by operating a market garden on the edge of the moors where he had the use of a powerful telescope erected on his land. Indoors he gave magic-lantern shows of the heavens and their constellations, and on clear evenings at the dark of the year we were invited to view the rings around Saturn, the beauty of the Milky Way or the craters and valleys of the Moon. After carefully sighting the objects he turned to us solemnly, "Sithee, lasses, isn't that a marvelous seet; a stupendous universe, yet we fritter our lives away i' wars and petty spites!" As youngsters we gazed, inclined to giggle; then came a moment of silent awe as awareness of "night clad in the beauty of a thousand inauspicious stars—the vast of night and its void"—seeped into consciousness.[26]

Perhaps Foley's radicalization included acquiring new beliefs about desirable political and social outcomes. But it began in the contemplation of things that had nothing to do with politics, things in themselves utterly useless, though within which it was possible to find a fuller sort of humanity than ordinary life offered. And yet surely gazing at the heavens did not determine Foley's destiny as a socialist. The freedom from small utilities and large ones, from colorless surroundings, from the human diminishment offered in given social roles—this freedom grounds a vast variety of human possibilities.

Freedom and Aspiration

Ought every use of the intellect for a social purpose be thought of as delusive and shallow? In our fear of resembling Strepsiades or Elena Greco at her social-climbing worst, should we emulate the pure uselessness of Aristophanes' Socrates, choosing intellectual projects that will be certain to provide no one with any good whatsoever?

It is true that if we treasure freedom from the self-interested conclusion and the agenda-driven hope, we find it most easily where our interests are least at stake—say, in the study of ancient mathematics or in philosophical inquiry into the nature of time. So, too, real inquiry may be impossible when our cares and interests are near to the surface, when our thoughts have been frozen in place thanks to the anxiety provoked by broad and open disagreement. We sometimes imagine that intellectual work can open room for conversation and communion on hot-button topics, but such attempts are rarely successful.

The social use of intellectual life lies in its cultivation of broader and richer ways of being human, in shaping our aspirations and our hopes for ourselves. It is obvious and widely noticed that literature provides a broadening of our perspective: we sympathize in our imaginations with human beings different from us—people of different races, genders, religions, times, and places. But the same is true of mathematics and science. It is surely part of what it means to be a human being to think mathematically and scientifically; by studying these subjects, especially through the thinkers of the past, we see from the inside magnificent and strange human possibilities and modes of comprehension.

When I say that intellectual life cultivates our aspirations, I do not mean that it expands career choices, although of course it may do that. We may discover a desire to be a firefighter or a forest ranger through exercising the love of learning. We may decide to leave everything to live in a poor hut outside the village, growing vegetables, praying, and offering spiritual advice when asked. But human aspiration is deeper in range and broader in scope than our outward life. We aspire to ways of *being*: to be wise, or kind; to be vast in understanding, steadfast in truth, humble in success, witty in adversity. Albert Schweitzer, who left a brilliant career in divinity and music to provide medical care to the poor in Africa, pointed out that not everyone has the opportunity to make such a dramatic and costly choice.[27] But anyone furnished with the basic necessities of life can aspire to the splendor of humanity, even if his or her individual splendor is not widely known or recognized.

The cultivation of modes of human aspiration must be undertaken freely and spontaneously; the intellect must be left to lead us where it leads us, regardless of what we thought our goals to be when we started. When young Augustine begins his search for wisdom he does not imagine sacrificing his girlfriend or his career in rhetoric. The intellect provides an intrinsically unpredictable *guide to life*, one with its own integrity and independence. If it is wholly subjugated to economic interests, whether personal or public, it will rationalize preexisting agendas rather than reshape them. If it is subjugated to the pursuit of justice, the agendas may be more appealing to some, but the result will be the same. The political agenda will dominate and obscure, making it difficult to evaluate our principles, to understand better and more deeply what justice is, to see it and its violations clearly before our eyes. The subjugation of the intellect will establish a hierarchy of moral experts who instruct others in partial truths. This is why intellectual life resists subservience to lesser goals such as wealth, ambition, politics, or pleasure. If intellectual life is not left to rest in its splendid uselessness, it will never bear its practical fruit. Likewise, the struggle for a just society is worthless if it costs us the fruits of justice.

The World of Learning and the Realm of Opinion

With the spirit of the age I am in complete disagreement, because it is filled with disdain for thinking.

—ALBERT SCHWEITZER, *OUT OF MY LIFE AND THOUGHT*

The exercise of the love of learning is a form of the inner life; it requires withdrawal from the pursuit of wealth and status, from politics and the pursuit of justice. Thanks to its withdrawn and inward character, it shines in beauty in difficult circumstances: the diminishment offered in given social roles, failure to catch onto a cog in the achievement machine, oppression and imprisonment, the suffusion of social life with self-serving falsehoods. It uncovers a human being who is not reducible to his or her economic, social, or political contributions.

Our external circumstances play on interior motivations: a conformist social environment appeals to our own desire to fit in socially; a competitive environment fuels our desires to achieve, to win honors, wealth, and status; poverty, deprivation, or oppression provokes our desire to be overwhelmed by physical or psychological suffering, or to minimize that suffering by cooperating with our captors or oppressors. So too a culture saturated with spectacles appeals to our desire to experience for the sake of experiencing, to dwell at the surfaces of things, to seek out a false communion with others that consists in being mutually spectators and spectacle. We can withdraw from the world, so to speak, and enter a realm of empty thrill seeking.

It seemed at first that intellectual life was a sort of exit: a retreat into the hidden room; a withdrawal into the cloister of the patent office, the concrete prison walls, the desert in the heart. But lovers of learning in fact seek after reality, more and more of it. Infused with seriousness, they seek to get to the bottom of life, to happiness, joy in the truth—or just plain truth, if there is no joy in it. Lila Cerullo is more plugged into the world—understood now as the real world—than are her violent neighbors, restlessly gaining territory and eliminating rivals. They pretend at control; they seek to conquer death by being one step ahead of it, whereas Lila ponders and loves and knows that these actions are all that matter.

Is immersion in "the world" in our original sense, the locus of the pursuit of status and wealth, in the end much different from a compulsion to watch gladiator matches, or to devote one's life to social media? It is, because reality has a better chance to break through. We may take a job for its prestige and discover that it serves a real need in our community, a service that we find fulfilling. We may look into the eyes of our trophy wife or trophy husband and all at once recognize the riches and the depths of another human being. We may enter academic life to aggrandize ourselves and to humiliate our family of origin, but we may fall in love with our subject along the way, or with the way that the subject affects our students. The world of our experience exposes us to real goods, but it takes a constant effort to see them clearly and to seek them out effectively. The danger of ambition is not so much selfishness as it is superficiality, the thrill of recognition, the joy of winning favor, the delight in making a splash. The thrills can hold us at the surfaces, keeping us from reaching for the real goods that lie past them.

Our Opinionized Universities

> Education is not in reality what some people proclaim it to be in their professions. What they aver is that they can put true knowledge into a soul that does not possess it, as if they were inserting vision into blind eyes. . . . But the true analogy . . . is that of an eye that could not be converted to the light from the darkness without turning the whole body.
>
> —PLATO, *REPUBLIC*, TRANS. PAUL SHOREY

If intellectual life essentially involves a reaching out past the surface, a questioning of appearances, a longing for more than is evident, then it has next to nothing to do with what is commonly called "knowledge"—the absorption of correct opinions. And yet correct opinions are what our contemporary intellectual institutions traffic in: the correct opinions about literature, or history, or science, or mathematics. Hence the universality of the bullet point, delivered in a college lecture, whose temporary memorization is the condition for the above-average grade. Hence too the administrative emphasis on learning outcomes; hence the politicization of everything, the reduction of learning to its social and political results.

My coreligionists, Catholics specifically and Christians more broadly, have also fallen into the trap of educating by opinions: riven by anxiety about the broader, hostile culture or by conflicts within their ranks, they each retreat to their own faction and turn to the rigid promotion of factional teachings. In this way they reduce serious inquiry and intellectual development to catechesis and evangelization by bullet points. The educational agenda is set more by broad political goals—to each faction its own—rather than by the fundamentals of spiritual life. We teach self-justifying arguments rather than the common human bonds that ground persuasion. We need to remind ourselves that Christianity has a few basics and holds out the prospect of free, vast, and indefinite growth in understanding and in sanctity. Christian teaching is less a containable artificial lake than it is an inexhaustible spring.

The authentic love of learning is not the exclusive property of Christians, of course. I have emphasized here what might be called the natural love of learning, the love of learning that belongs to all human beings by their nature, which provides a natural good, one that can in turn be elevated by grace. That this elevation is possible ought to inspire intellectual Christians to promote the love of learning broadly, in accordance with the old slogan that grace builds on nature.

So too at secular institutions, much of what counts as education in the contemporary scene is the cultivation of correct opinions. Some is the much-maligned education supported by progressive activists, education that seeks primarily social and political results rather than the cultivation of free, thoughtful human beings. Some is the conservative mirror image of progressive activism: the promotion of correct opinions about free markets or economic liberty, again with an eye to broad political results.

In reaction to the widespread ideological narrowing of education, old-school small-*l* liberals promote viewpoint diversity, the civil exchange of differing opinions. Even this school celebrates the same false god as the others: opinionating, the holding of a viewpoint. Forming an opinion has as little to do with inquiry as correctness has to do with knowledge of truth. Thus the promotion of viewpoint diversity is nearly as superficial and dehumanizing as the forms of indoctrination it means to replace. When we debate a given topic we devise yet more effective rationalizations for what we already believe. A debate rarely spurs an earnest launch into the depths of things—not, at any rate, with the effectiveness of a good book, a fundamental human question, or an intense and open-ended conversation. A selection of viewpoints does not imply nor can it replace the virtue of seriousness.

The civil exchange of opinions can create a veneer of tolerance, but it requires no serious thinking. Opinions rarely change. Nor, when they do, is their change necessarily the sign of any intellectual engagement. Opinions are fixed in place by a network of socially directed impulses of fear and ambition. We change our minds when we change our clique, our social circle. At the level of opinion, our reasoning powers operate backward to justify predetermined choices. Our social world is our intellectual comfort zone. To break its bonds, so as to actually learn something, requires a sort of intellectual violence: the pain inflicted by a torturously realistic book, by an unanswerable question, or by the presence of an intelligent human being who is oriented differently than we are.

Any reader of Plato's *Republic* remembers that the realm of opinion is compared to a shadowy cavern, and that a difficult, painful conversion is needed to begin real intellectual work. The turning around from shadows into light begins by facing fundamental questions. What makes a community just? Is there an order to the natural world? What are mathematical objects? Is a human being more like a beast or a god? Questions like these shatter opinions and force us into real conversation with the voices of the past and with one another.

Our educational institutions as they are, dedicated to the largely anonymous transmission of correct opinions or to exchanges of ideas that do not get down to fundamental questions, have chosen to short-cut the deep bonds of human unity for the narrow, the superficial, the political, and the divisive. In this way they cut off the dissatisfaction necessary to cultivate aspirations, settling instead for the short-term satisfaction of holding a view.

An excellent book, like a fundamental question, confounds us. We find Don Quixote ridiculous while overcome with affection and admiration for him. We despise Fanny Price, the protagonist of *Mansfield Park*, while being forced to recognize her virtue. Enter deeply into the historical past, and we slow down our rush to judgment of lost cultures steeped in evil. The slave owner and the Nazi show their human colors, and we begin to see ourselves in them, to wonder what sorts of evil we ourselves may be steeped in.

Whereas in good literature or in historical inquiry our sympathies are put on the rack, in mathematics or science we face the limits of our ability to draw conclusions. We are able only with difficulty to untangle organic molecules or to prove Gödel's incompleteness theorem. We find it flatly impossible to give an account of how an electron can be both a particle and a wave, or how a geometric point can be both something and nothing.

Our desires for truth and understanding, driven on by both frustration and awe, bear us into the depths of the intellect where real learning takes place. But natural to us as these desires are, they fight against the other desires I have described: inbuilt sloth, the thrill of the spectacle, the easy rush of outrage, the drive for status or achievement, and the uneasy fortress of comfort given by belonging to a particular social group.

The love of learning faces competition with many other human elements, our desires for the surfaces. Accordingly, to cultivate it requires rules of discipline, so that the difficult things are made easier and easy things more difficult. Politics on campus should be rare, and almost always extracurricular. One ought to be thrown together with disparate social groups to learn collaboratively. Open-ended inquiry, rather than rationalizing to suit preexisting conclusions, ought to be central.

The diminishment of intellectual life caused by the opinionization of everything also demeans our students. If we cultivate our college campuses either as echo chambers or as chocolate-box assortments of viewpoints, we think of young people first and foremost as receptacles of opinions, as consumers of content, and as subjects whose experiences must be carefully managed. The difference is only whether the selection of opinions is curated by concerned officials or left to the open market, where gimmicky appeals or social pressures might draw in fresh consumers. Either way, we deny the rational agency and inbuilt love of learning of our students. We seek to control the reactions of beings viewed as inferior to us rather than to undertake an open-ended inquiry with fellow free adults.

Free adults who undertake sustained and serious inquiry are not made from scratch—they are cultivated on trust. Education begins from the assumption that students are capable of taking responsibility for their own learning and that they are naturally motivated, even driven from within to pursue fundamental questions. That assumption is based on nothing other than the simple humanity of the student and the student's free choice to take up an education.

It is a commonplace of the theory of human excellence, going back at least to Aristotle, that virtues are learned by imitation. If we wish to promote the virtue of seriousness in young people, to pass on free inquiry, to lead students into the depths where real insight and understanding take place, we must first cultivate ourselves. We should remind ourselves of the human questions that once gripped us. We should reconsider our work, our choices, the broad scope of our lives in light of those questions.

We must form the community of equals that human seriousness makes possible, and invite our students to join us.

Habits and disciplines are transmitted person to person, with mutual rapt attention, fed by appropriate encouragement or discouragement. If we wish to learn how to play the piano, or to make furniture, or to practice the martial arts, we seek out and follow a master. It is a disgrace to our system of higher education that person-to-person teaching belongs only to a handful of liberal arts colleges and to elite doctoral programs. Our campuses burgeon with new buildings, food courts, and climbing walls; as class sizes become larger, the distance between teacher and student becomes wider, and the quality of the education less and less serious. Somehow learning is imagined as something that could be boiled down to the mastery of a set of sentences. There are useful subjects that can be learned this way, but nothing that would justify the expense or the inconvenience of a modern university.

Restoring Our Humanity

How vainly men themselves amaze
To win the Palm, the Oke, or Bayes;
And their uncessant Labours see
Crown'd from some single Herb or Tree,
Whose short and narrow verged Shade
Does prudently their toils upbraid;
While all Flow'rs and all Trees do close
To weave the Garlands of repose.

—ANDREW MARVELL, "THE GARDEN"

As I wrote in my prologue, I thought intensely about the value of learning in order to find my own place in the world, and so I made a decision for myself to return to person-to-person teaching. But I started writing about the importance of the work of the mind as a response to the accelerated decline in which I found academic institutions and my academic friends upon returning to "the world": humanities departments and institutions closing, teaching jobs disappearing, class sizes ballooning, and my academic friends at various stages of disillusion or discouragement, afraid that their work was ultimately insignificant.

What I saw and still see has in fact been going on for many years. For some time, intellectual institutions in the United States have been under significant financial and political pressure to abandon education for programs with economic or political uses. What are called "the humanities" have suffered particularly, but not exclusively. I will not here go into the various social and economic causes or propose much in the way of practical policies. I give only the following very simple and partial diagnosis: we academic professionals have lost touch with our origins in ordinary human intellectual activity. We have thus lost the capacity to justify and explain to our fellow citizens or to philanthropists—much less to ourselves—why our institutions matter.

Not long ago, I came across a hundred-year-old scholarly edition of the *Annals* of Sennacherib, the Assyrian emperor of the eighth century BCE. The annals of the Assyrian kings are fascinating for their gruesome violence, their radiant confidence in God's favor, their subsumption of the collective under the individual leader, their view that any act in their kingdom is an act of the king. The introduction broached the human question most evidently raised by the work—the corrupting force of absolute military and political power:

History begins with the vanity of kings. (Will it end with the vanity of the demos?)[28]

Scholars today are both too sophisticated and too diffident to appeal to such an obvious, profound, and universal question in a work meant for specialists. They hide the human under jargon, or lose sight of it altogether. A contemporary scholar might begin:

> The textual sources for the construction of the notion of kingship in the Neo-Assyrian period are well known but undertheorized.

When scholars write for a general audience, they assume that readers care only for current events and celebrities. So the modern book on Sennacherib for the general audience might begin:

> In the spring of 2015, ISIS destroyed the ancient Assyrian city of Nimrud. Actor George Clooney condemned the destruction as "an outrage."[29]

Providing background for the news is of course important. But it does not exhaust the human interest of the past. The invocation of images of bloodthirsty terrorists and concerned celebrities is not needed to make history interesting. Ordinary people care about the eternal things as well—the vanity of kings, the horrors of war.

Our institutions have also lost touch in other respects. Colleges and universities once held central a practice whose success was evident and that therefore provided an endless source of confidence. That practice is called teaching, and it consists in the person-to-person transmission of the habits of mind that underlie all serious thinking, reflection, and discovery. Good teaching is manifest to those who receive it, and it thus inspires a sometimes absurd gratitude; so too, its value is abundantly evident to those who practice it. It has nearly disappeared from our college campuses, surviving only thanks to hardy, dedicated, principled individuals, who eke out their beautiful work without recognition or adequate recompense. Meanwhile, high-prestige academics compete for the jobs in which they can teach least and travel to Europe and Asia most. They produce reams of research, much of it completely disconnected from any recognizable human question. All the same, since publication seems somehow quantifiable, it meets administrative demands for measurable outcomes. So high-achieving professors are rewarded with six-figure salaries and what passes for names in lights. Even intellectually fervent and morally conscious academics are understandably helpless in the face of this set of incentives, as helpless as a natural lover of learning faced with an intoxicating series of straight As. The reward, by nature, becomes the goal.

Elite academics make up only a tiny percentage of university teachers. It is widely known that professors have been slowly and silently replaced with adjuncts, a slave class of teachers who must teach vast numbers of students at a time in order to scrape by with wages and benefits one might find in the fast-food industry. As of 2016, these adjuncts made up almost three-quarters of university teachers in the United States.[30] Given such high loads of courses and students, and given the additional strain of poverty, adequate teaching is virtually impossible. Neither sober and guilt-laden think pieces by elite academics nor cris de coeur by these frequently brilliant and dedicated teachers themselves have done anything whatsoever to halt or even to slow the destruction of university teaching. Legislators piling on regulations, student-consumers with absurd demands for expensive campus playgrounds, and administrators with allegiance to hostile principles from the business world deserve some of the blame. But elite professors, small though they be in number, have a great deal of power that they choose daily not to use. They choose to be content providers in anonymous classrooms, and they choose not to fight to preserve or to restore the quality of the education that they themselves received as students. Moreover, adjunct professors themselves need to ask whether the thin icing of prestige given by university teaching is the best use of their considerable intellectual and pastoral talent.

It is my hope that our institutions that support intellectual activity will recover their original purpose, as they need to in order to flourish. Institutional design, especially the structure of incentives and rewards, has an enormous effect on our ultimate ends, what is easy for us to choose, what we enjoy, what we value. It deserves to be the focus of hard thinking at this moment of crisis. But the account of the forms and practices of learning here is meant to be more general. Our intellectual institutions may decay and collapse, but intellectual life itself cannot be allowed to follow. We must reconnect with and remind ourselves of what matters in what we do, so that this particularly human way of being, its joys and sorrows, its modes of excellence, and its unique bonds of communion, is not lost.

Epilogue
THE EVERYDAY INTELLECTUAL

As for me, my bed is made: I am against bigness and greatness in all their forms, and with the invisible molecular forces that work from individual to individual, stealing in through the crannies of the world like so many soft rootlets, or like the capillary oozing of water, and yet rending the hardest monuments of men's pride, if you give them time. The bigger the unit you deal with, the hollower, the more brutal, the more mendacious is the life displayed. So I am against all big organizations as such, national ones first and foremost; against all big successes and big results; and in favor of the eternal forces of truth which always work in the individual and immediately unsuccessful way, under-dogs always, till history comes, long after they are dead, and puts them on the top.

—WILLIAM JAMES, LETTER TO MRS. HENRY
WHITMAN, JUNE 7, 1899

Not long ago it was widely taken for granted that intellectual activity benefited ordinary people. I mentioned earlier the classic handbooks of the early twentieth century *How to Live on 24 Hours a Day* and *The Intellectual Life*. To nonacademics with intellectual interests, ordinary people, those little books offered a wealth of practical advice for their intellectual work along with soaring rhetoric to inspire and encourage them. These authors wrote as a great flood of translations of classics were being published in inexpensive editions.

The early twentieth century had its powerful, hard-nosed advocates of practice over theory and its fantasy-driven evangelists of technology. Still, it seems evident that in the age of Everyman's Library and reading clubs at the Mechanics Institute, publishers, academics, and grassroots organizers built and defended forms of intellectual life that went to the bottom of things and reached out to the broadest of audiences. Even the activists of the early twentieth century did homage to the democracy of serious inquiry: Marxists went to the poorest areas and taught to anyone who would listen intricacies of Hegel and Feuerbach that a modern-day professor would tremble to assign to undergraduates.

In the face of these examples, to justify intellectual activity in terms of its economic and political benefits, as do contemporary defenders of the humanities and liberal education, might seem banal or beside the point. But such defenses are worse than that: they are false and destructively so. For intellectual life to deliver the human benefit it provides, it must be in fact withdrawn from considerations of economic benefit or of social and political efficacy. This is the case in part because, as the little human things testify, a human being is more than an instrument of personal or public benefit. Intellectual life is a source of human dignity exactly because it is something beyond politics and social life. But withdrawal from the world is also necessary because intellectual life is, as I have said, an ascetic practice.

If intellectual life is not an elite property but a piece of the human heritage, it belongs first and fundamentally to ordinary human beings. All intellectual life, no matter how ultimately sophisticated, originates in the human questions arising in and behind ordinary life. Scholarship is exciting in its own right, but it means nothing in a world where there is no first-order reflection, no ordinary thinking about human nature or the structure and origins of the world. Higher study is pointless if literature or philosophy or mathematics or the nature of nature has ultimately nothing to do with the human good of ordinary people or with paths of understanding one might follow in daily life. So, too, scholarship is owed back in return to ordinary people, in forms of outreach that respect the role of a free intellect in a good human life.

Anyone seeking a good human life benefits from learning in all of its breadth and depth. Nor need one work in a university or attend one to cultivate the virtue of seriousness. Zeal for the fundamentals in life is fueled by aspiration, by imagining forms of human life that we wish to inhabit or become. Our intellectual culture prizes destruction over edification, a thrill of superiority over deep encouragement, and the reinforcement of factional loyalties over common ground. Yet any thoughtful person, not to speak of a writer, artist, critic, or journalist, can seek out examples, living and dead, historical and fictional, of human beings who have strained every nerve to seek more, better, finer, nobler ways of living.

In this book I have been forced to use mostly examples of high achievers in the realm of the intellect: Einstein, Gramsci, Goethe, Augustine. That is because these are the modes of intellectual life one can easily find in a library—the high achievers are worthy of books. One of the diseases of our spectacle-riddled culture is that we forget that the invisible life has all the human splendor of the visible one, and often more. I have had in mind all along, and have appealed to where possible, the humble bookworm, the amateur naturalist, the contemplative taxi driver. If you, like me, are naturally drawn to achievement, collect examples of ordinary thinkers—human beings whose splendor is known only to a few, their family, their neighbors, their coworkers. Settle back in awe from time to time, as I do, in thinking about the vast treasury of thought and experience that will never be available to us.

Let us remind ourselves of the broad scope of human enterprise as well as the depths available to anyone with a bit of time to think. Let us give free play to the human intellect and the human imagination, in an attempt to ground all that is in our hearts in what matters most.

ACKNOWLEDGMENTS

In this book I have tried to articulate what I have learned about intellectual life over the course of my own life. To properly acknowledge my debts in this experiential learning process would be tantamount to acknowledging the debts I owe for my life in general. It must suffice to say that I am grateful beyond words to all of the communities that have nurtured this activity in me, and to the teachers, students, and colleagues who made them up. But it all began with birth and childhood, and so I dedicate this book to my brothers and to our parents, with gratitude.

———

The book properly speaking began life as a fifteen-minute presentation with slides at the fall conference of the Center for Ethics and Culture at the University of Notre Dame in 2015. I was helped in assembling and thinking through the images for the talk by Marianne Thompson, who provided original illustrations of the philosopher's withdrawal from the world. The talk (called "Freedom and Intellectual Life") was published online a few months later at *First Things*, and a version of it appears here in the first chapter. I owe a special debt to the audience at the talk and to the readers of the initial essay, especially those who wrote to me. Their enthusiasm encouraged me to think that others, too, felt a need for a robust account of why learning matters for its own sake, and that this need stretched across political and religious lines. The late Peter Lawler invited me to write "Why Intellectual Work Matters," for *Modern Age*, which also shares material with different parts of the book. My friends among the Dominican friars, especially Fr. John Corbett, OP, Fr. Michael Sherwin, OP, and Fr. Thomas Joseph White, OP, responded with special enthusiasm to my attempts to describe the natural good of learning, and their efforts through the Thomistic Institute have permitted me to share versions of these thoughts with Catholic college students over the past two years.

It was Rob Tempio's idea to write a book on the topic of the essay, and Rob has remained a constant source of enthusiasm, encouragement, interesting ideas, and basic help from start to finish. This book would not have come into the world without him.

The bulk of the work on the manuscript was accomplished thanks to a generous fellowship from the Center for Ethics and Culture. I am very grateful to its staff, especially to Carter Snead, Ryan Madison, and Margaret Cabaniss, for their faithful support, and to my dean, Joe MacFarland, for making it possible for me to take a semester away from teaching. Jim Hankins, my colleague at the center, shared with me his parallel work on humanism in the Renaissance, and put me on the trail of many helpful references and examples. I learned more, and more pleasantly, from weekly lunches with Jim than from many visits to the library. While at Notre Dame I also enjoyed the support of members of the philosophy department—especially Sean Kelsey, who loaned me his office; Meghan Sullivan; Katharina Kraus; and David O'Connor. I am deeply grateful as well for the joyful hospitality of the residents of Sibley House.

The final preparation of the manuscript was funded by a National Endowment for the Humanities Summer Stipend. Any views, findings, conclusions, or recommendations expressed in this book do not necessarily reflect those of the National Endowment for the Humanities.

I am very much indebted to my students at St. John's College over the past several years with whom I have had such stimulating and fruitful conversations about the books and authors I discuss, as well as to my teachers who introduced our reading list to me here a quarter-century ago. Special thanks must also go to my seminar partners, (Nina Haigney, Robert Druecker, Bill Braithwaite, and Michael Comenetz), from whom I have learned a great deal and whose insights into the books I suspect appear in digested and adulterated forms in these pages. Two fruitful summer reading groups with my colleagues on Ferrante's Neapolitan novels helped me greatly in thinking about those books. So did another reading group of colleagues and students on Aristophanes' *Clouds*. At St. John's, no two humans think alike about why our program of study is valuable. I am deeply indebted to the college, but I am not qualified to speak on its behalf, and my views should not be mistaken for those of anyone there in either official or unofficial capacity, apart from myself.

Several friends passed on key tips, parallel treatments, or juicy passages. Aline Gram shared with me her beautiful work on Dorothy Day, and Maria Surat looked over the Day section. I received advice from Stephen Menn and Janice Thompson (on Augustine), Cristina Ionescu (on Romanian political prisoners), and Fr. Aaron Qureshi (on mathematics in prison). Robert Abbott, Gisela Berns, Katharina Kraus, and Cary and Susan Stickney, helped me with Goethe and Gramsci. Olivia Crosby was a steadfast source of excitement and support.

Anton Barba-Kay, Agnes Callard, and Rachel Singpurwalla read partial drafts of the manuscript, and gave me very helpful feedback. A long afternoon's conversation with Agnes about the book helped to pull me out of a pit of discouragement. Peter Wicks read the manuscript and saved me from many stylistic problems. Kris McDaniel read an entire draft at very short notice, and put me under pressure to clarify the philosophically muddy portions. (That they remain muddy is, of course, not his fault.) Nina Haigney and Jim Hankins also read the first version and offered crucial advice and encouragement. The two anonymous readers for Princeton provided excellent, thorough, and philosophically challenging suggestions, and I'm grateful for their pressuring me to make the religious aspects of my thinking more explicit. The manuscript was swiftly and beautifully edited by Alice Falk. Without the sacrifice of their time that all these readers offered, this book would not have been possible.

I am most profoundly grateful to all from whom I entreated prayers for this project, and especially for the prayers of Saint Martin de Porres and the Mother of God, the book's special patrons.

NOTES

Prologue

1. Translations are my own unless otherwise noted.

Introduction

1. I recommend the examples collected in David Graeber's recent book, *Bullshit Jobs* (New York: Simon and Schuster, 2018).

2. Steve Martin, *Born Standing Up* (New York: Simon and Schuster, 2007), 64–65.

3. See Plato, *Republic* 2, 357b–358a. Aristotle gives his account of the highest end—happiness, or *eudaimonia*—along with an account of the structure of human ends, in the first seven chapters of the *Nicomachean Ethics*. He argues that the highest end of human life is contemplation in *Nicomachean Ethics* 10.6–8.

4. See Jonathan Rose, *The Intellectual Life of the British Working Classes* (New Haven, CT: Yale University Press, 2001). For an account of the migration of the British movement to the United States, see Scott Buchanan, "Awakening the Seven Sleepers," in *Scott Buchanan: A Centennial Appreciation of His Life and Work, 1895–1968*, ed. Charles A. Nelson (Annapolis: St. John's College Press, 1995), 1–13.

5. A. G. Sertillanges, OP, *The Intellectual Life: Its Spirit, Conditions, Methods*, trans. Mary Ryan (Washington, DC: Catholic University Press, 1987).

6. Arnold Bennett, *How to Live on 24 Hours a Day* (Garden City, NY: Doubleday, 1910).

7. Jack London, *Martin Eden* (New York: Holt, Rinehart, and Winston, 1908), 137.

8. George Orwell, *Down and Out in Paris and London* (New York: Harcourt, 1933), 105–21.

9. Barbara Ehrenreich, *Nickeled and Dimed: On (Not) Getting By in America* (New York: Picador, 2001), 46.

10. James Bloodworth, *Hired: Six Months Undercover in Low-Wage Britain* (London: Atlantic Books, 2018), 11–76.

11. Bloodworth, 51.

12. Plato, *Theaetetus* 172d–e, trans. M. J. Levett (Indianapolis, IN: Hackett, 1990).

13. Lauren Smiley, "The Shut-In Economy," *Medium*, March 25, 2015, https://medium.com/matter/the-shut-in-economy-ec3ec1294816.

14. See Tom Slater's essay on our voluntary submission to "Little Brother": "Selfie-Surveillance: Who Needs Big Brother when We Constantly Film Ourselves?" *Spectator*, June 1, 2019, https://www.spectator.co.uk/2019/06/selfie-surveillance-who-needs-big-brother-when-we-constantly-film-ourselves.

15. *New York Times* obituary, August 3, 1955, 23.

16. John Ashbery, introduction to *The Collected Poems of Frank O'Hara*, ed. Donald Allen (Berkeley: University of California Press, 1971), vii.

17. I rely on the account of Kober's life and work in Margalit Fox, *The Riddle of the Labyrinth: The Quest to Crack an Ancient Code* (New York: HarperCollins, 2013).

18. See Ernst Kantorowicz, *Frederick the Second, 1194–1250*, trans. E. O. Lorimer (New York: Ungar, 1957).

19. Victor Frankl, *Man's Search for Meaning* (Boston, MA: Beacon, 1959).

20. Kareem Shaheen and Ian Black, "Beheaded Syrian Scholar Refuses to Lead Isis to Hidden Palmyra Antiquities," *Guardian*, August 19, 2015, https://www.theguardian.com/world/2015/aug/18/isis-beheads-archaeologist-syria.

21. Simone Weil, "La vie syndicale: en marge du Comité d'études" [Trade union life: notes on the Committee for Instruction], *L'Effort*, December 19, 1931, cited in Simone Petrement, *Simone Weil: A Life*, trans. Raymond Rosenthal (New York: Pantheon, 1976), 87–88.

22. Mendel Nun's museum, the House of Anchors, can still be visited at Kibbutz Ein Gev in the Galilee. His life is briefly described here: https://www.jerusalemperspective.com/author/mendel-nun/.

Chapter 1

1. A version of this section appeared as "Freedom and Intellectual Life," *First Things*, April 7, 2016.

2. France: Les Films des Tournelles, 2009.

3. West Germany: Filmverlag der Autoren, 1974.

4. Plato, *Symposium* 174d–175b

5. Plutarch, *Life of Marcellus* 19.

6. Valerius Maximus, *Memorable Deeds and Sayings* 8.7.

7. Anonymous, *Dialogue between Mary and Joseph*, in Sebastian P. Brock, "Mary and the Angel, and Other Syriac Dialogue Poems," *Marianum* 68 (2006): 134.

8. Ambrose, *Concerning Virgins* II.2.10, trans. H. de Romestin, E. de Romestin, and H.T.F. Duckworth, in *Nicene and Post-Nicene Fathers, Second Series*, vol. 10, ed. Philip Schaff and Henry Wace (Buffalo, NY: Christian Literature, 1896). This is the oldest

appearance of the image of Mary reading when the angel arrives that I have been able to discover.

9. Augustine, sermon 196.1, trans. Edmund Hill, OP, and John E. Rotelle, OSA, in *Sermons of St. Augustine*, vol. 6 (Hyde Park, NY: New City, 1990).

10. Augustine, sermon 191.4, trans. Hill and Rotelle, in *Sermons*, vol. 6.

11. Einstein, letter to Michele Besso, December 12, 1919, trans. and cited in W. Isaacson, *Einstein: His Life and Universe* (New York: Simon and Schuster, 2008), 78.

12. Einstein, *Autobiographical Notes*, in *Albert Einstein: Philosopher-Scientist*, ed. P. A. Schlipp (Lasalle, IL: Open Court, 1969), 1:17–18.

13. Following the account of Albrecht Fölsing, *Albert Einstein: A Biography*, trans. Ewald Osers (New York: Viking, 1997), 70–112.

14. Maja Einstein, "Albert Einstein: A Biographical Sketch," in *The Collected Papers of Albert Einstein, English Translation*, trans. Anna Beck (Princeton, NJ: Princeton University Press, 1987), 1:xxii.

15. The lives of Einstein and Fritz Haber, and their friendship, are discussed in Fritz Stern, "Albert Einstein and Fritz Haber," in *Einstein's German World* (Princeton, NJ: Princeton University Press, 1999), 59–164.

16. Einstein, letter to Heinrich Zanger, *ca.* April 10, 1915, trans. in *Einstein on Politics*, ed. David Rowe and Robert Schulman (Princeton, NJ: Princeton University Press, 2007), 67.

17. J. J. O' Connor and E. F. Robertson, "Andre Weil," MacTutor History of Mathematics archive, St. Andrews University, 2014, http://www-history.mcs.st-andrews.ac .uk/Biographies/Weil.html. See also the account of these events (without an account of the mathematical discoveries) in Petrement, *Simone Weil*, 366–72.

18. "André Weil Writes from Rouen Prison," letter to Eveline Weil, MacTutor History of Mathematics archive, St. Andrews University, 2008, http://www-history.mcs .st-andrews.ac.uk/Extras/Weil_prison.html.

19. Translation by Manuel S. Almeida Rodriguez, in his "Some Notes on the Tragic Writing of Antonio Gramsci," *International Gramsci Journal* 1, no. 2 (2010): 10. An account of Gramsci's life in prison is found in *Selections from the Prison Notebooks of Antonio Gramsci*, ed. and trans. Q. Hoare and G. N. Smith (New York: International, 1971), lxxxix–xciv.

20. Reported in Gramsci, *Prison Notebooks*, lxxxix.

21. I draw on *The Autobiography of Malcolm X: As Told to Alex Haley* (New York: Ballantine Books, 1964), with details clarified and verified by Manning Marable, *Malcolm X: A Life of Reinvention* (New York: Viking, 2011).

22. Malcolm X, *Autobiography*, 196.

23. Letter to Philbert Little, February 4, 1949, quoted in Marable, *Malcolm X*, 92.

24. Letter to Reverend Samuel L. Laviscount, November 14, 1950, quoted in Marable, 95.

25. Malcolm X, *Autobiography*, 387.

26. Marable, *Malcolm X*, presents the evidence (13, 433–34, and ch. 16).

27. Augustine, *On Free Will*, trans. Thomas Williams (Indianapolis: Hackett, 1993), 2.16.

28. Augustine, *Confessions* 10.8.15. All translations of the *Confessions* from Augustine's *Confessions*, 2nd ed., trans. F. J. Sheed, ed. with notes by M. P. Foley (Indianapolis: Hackett, 2006).

29. I rely here on the account of Richard Holmes, *The Age of Wonder* (London: Harper, 2008), ch. 2 and 4.

30. For Goethe's life and general scientific practice, I was greatly helped by the materials collected in Matthew Bell's *The Essential Goethe*, and by Bell's introduction (Princeton, NJ: Princeton University Press, 2016).

31. For what I understand of Goethe's botany, I am indebted to my colleagues who taught in the freshman laboratory sequence at St. John's from 2015 to 2017, as well as to helpful discussions of the *Metamorphosis* with my students over those two academic years.

32. J. W. Goethe, *Italian Journey [1786–88]*, trans. W. H. Auden and Elizabeth Meyer (Berkeley, CA: North Point, 1982), 363.

33. As reported in Goethe's *Truth and Poetry from My Own Life*, ed. Parke Godwin (London: George Bell, 1906), 2:210.

34. Bell, *Essential Goethe*, 1003.

35. Goethe, *Italian Journey*, 54.

36. See Hetty Saunders, *My House of Sky: The Life and Work of J.A. Baker* (Toller Fratrum, UK: Little Toller Books, 2017).

37. I am grateful to the students in my senior language tutorial in the spring of 2019 for helpful discussions of *The Peregrine*.

38. John Baker, *The Peregrine* (New York: New York Review Books, 2005), 14.

39. Baker, 50–51.

40. Baker, 12.

41. Baker, 132.

42. George Steiner, *Real Presences* (Chicago: University of Chicago Press, 1989), 8.

43. Primo Levi, *The Periodic Table*, trans. R. Rosenthal (London: Penguin, 2000), 35.

44. Yves Simon, "Freedom in Daily Life," in *Freedom and Community*, ed. Charles P. O'Donnell (New York: Fordham, 1968), 5.

45. See Harry Frankfurt, "On Bullshit," in his *The Importance of What We Care About* (Cambridge: Cambridge University Press, 1988), reprinted as *On Bullshit* (Princeton, NJ: Princeton University Press, 2005).

46. Simon, *Freedom and Community*, 5–6.

47. Finley Peter Dunne, "The Food We Eat," in *Dissertations by Mr. Dooley* (New York: Harper, 1906), 247–54.

48. Simone Petrement, "The Year of Factory Work," in *Simone Weil*, 235.

49. As recorded in his extraordinary memoir, *Black Like Me* (New York: New American Library, 1960).

50. Catherine Doherty, *Poustinia* (Notre Dame, IN: Ave Maria, 1975), ch. 2.

51. One hopeful sign of revival is Chris Arnade's recent endeavor to immerse himself among the poorest of the American poor, as described in his book *Dignity: Seeking Respect in Back Row America* (New York: Sentinel, 2019).

52. Plato, *Apology* 28e, 32a–e, 30e–31b.

53. Saint John of the Cross, *The Ascent of Mount Carmel*, 3rd ed., ed. and trans. E. Allison Peers (Garden City, NY: Image, 1958), 1.2–1.3.

54. John of the Cross, *Ascent of Mount Carmel*, 1.3.4.

55. Discussed in Matthew Arnold, "The Study of Poetry," in *Essays in Criticism, Second Series* (London: Macmillan, 1888), 1–55, but perhaps more broadly and insightfully in Steiner, *Real Presences*.

56. Steiner, *Real Presences*.

57. Philip Roth, "Primo Levi," introduction to Levi, *Periodic Table*.

58. Irina Dumitrescu, "Poems in Prison: The Survival Strategies of Romanian Political Prisoners," in *Rumba under Fire: The Arts of Survival from West Point to Delhi*, ed. Dumitrescu (n.p.: Punctum Books, 2016), 15–30.

59. As described in her memoir, *Grey Is the Color of Hope*, trans. A. Kojevnikov (London: Hodder and Stoughton, 1988).

60. Louise Jury, "We Wrote a Letter to Yeltsin, and Then We Packed Our Bags," interview with Irina Ratushinskaya, *Independent* (London), June 6, 1999, http://www .independent.co.uk/arts-entertainment/we-wrote-a-letter-to-yeltsin-and-then-we -packed-our-bags-1098401.html.

61. Quoted in Rose, *Intellectual Life*, 127.

62. Rose, 127.

63. Rose, 45

64. W.E.B. Du Bois, *The Souls of Black Folk* (New York: Vintage/Library of America, 1990), 82.

65. Rose, *Intellectual Life*, 81.

66. Steiner, *Real Presences*, 12.

67. For case studies, see George Hutchinson's recent account of American literature in the 1940s: *Facing the Abyss: American Literature and Culture in the 1940s* (New York: Columbia University Press, 2018). Hutchinson argues that in that period authors from marginalized groups sought recognition *as human beings*.

68. José Maria Gironella, *The Cypresses Believe in God*, trans. H. de Onis (New York: Knopf, 1955).

69. For an account of Holstenius's territorial wrangling with Protestants, see Nicholas Hardy, *Criticism and Confession: The Bible in the Seventeenth Century Republic of Letters* (Oxford: Oxford University Press, 2017), 281–304. I am indebted to Jim Hankins for pointing out to me the example of Holstenius.

70. Quoted and cited by F.J.M. Blom in his "Lucas Holstenius (1596–1661) and England," on which I rely for this anecdote. In *Studies in Seventeenth Century English Literature: Festschrift for T.A. Birrell on the Occasion of His Sixtieth Birthday*, ed. G.A.M. Janssens and F.G.A.M. Aarts (Amsterdam: Editions Rotopi, 1984), 25–39.

Chapter 2

1. The story of Thales falling into the well is told in Plato, *Theaetetus* 174a, and analyzed at length by Hans Blumenberg in his *The Laughter of the Thracian Woman*, trans. Spencer Hawkins (New York: Bloomsbury, 2015). The tale of the olive presses appears in Aristotle, *Politics* 1, 1259a6–19, and is repeated in the *Life of Thales* by Diogenes Laertius, 26.

2. Plutarch, *Life of Marcellus* 14–17.

3. I owe this translation of φροντιστήριον to Abby Stuart.

4. Aristophanes, *Clouds* 229–30.

5. Plato, *Republic* 369b–374d.

6. At the end of *Republic* 5, that is; after the education of books 2 and 3 and the outlining of the major laws.

7. Pierre Bourdieu, *Distinction: A Social Critique of the Judgement of Taste*, trans. Richard Nice (Cambridge, MA: Harvard University Press, 1984).

8. Rose, *Intellectual Life*, 137–38.

9. Rose, 143–44.

10. Martin, *Born Standing Up*, 64–65.

11. Muriel Barbery, *The Elegance of the Hedgehog*, trans. Alison Anderson (New York: Europa editions, 2008).

12. As counted by question marks; see James J. O'Donnell, *Augustine, Confessions: Commentary on Books 1–7* (Oxford: Clarendon, 1992), 20.

13. As Peter Brown emphasizes; see his *Augustine of Hippo* (Berkeley: University of California, 1967), 169–72. I am indebted to Brown's book in many ways.

14. Augustine, *Confessions* 3.4.8.

15. Augustine 3.12.21.

16. Augustine 5.3.3–5.7.13.

17. Augustine 6.3.3.

18. Augustine 7.9.13.

19. See the extraordinary scene drawn in Brown's *Augustine of Hippo*, ch. 14, 138–39.

20. Augustine, *Confessions* 10.35.54.

21. Augustine 6.8.13.

22. Simon, *Freedom and Community*, 3–4.

23. Augustine, *Confessions* 10.35.55.

24. Augustine, *On Order (de Ordine)*, trans. S. Borruso (South Bend, IN: St. Augustine's Press, 2007), 1.8.26.

25. Augustine, *Confessions* 3.10.18. See explanatory note *ad loc.* in the Hackett edition, ed. M. P. Foley.

26. Augustine 10.23.33.

27. Augustine, *City of God* 22.12–20.

28. Augustine's own image in *Confessions* 3.2.4: "That is why I loved these sorrows, not that I wanted them to bite too deep (for I had no wish to suffer the sorrows I looked upon), yet, as if they had been fingernails, their scratching was followed by swelling and inflammation and sores with pus flowing. Such was my life, but was that a life, my God?"

29. Augustine 4.4.9.

30. Augustine 3.2.4.

31. Augustine 2.4.9–2.10.18.

32. Dante, *Inferno* 26.85–142.

33. Dante 26.112–17; see also 98.

34. The place where the distinction is perhaps clearest is *On the Usefulness of Believing* 9.22. Augustine also begins to make a distinction between the "curious" and the "studious" in a difficult passage of *On the Trinity* (10.1.3). It is the claim in the latter passage, that the curious person "wants to know everything," that inspires Paul Griffiths's interpretation of intellectual appetite gone wrong in his *Intellectual Appetite: A Theological Grammar* (Washington, DC: Catholic University Press, 2009). Griffiths is giving an account of a Christian love of learning; I am giving an account of the natural love of learning that I think (and I think Augustine agrees) is available to Christians and non-Christians alike. Thus my view of the love of learning is more optimistic than Griffiths's. Still, I was comforted and encouraged to learn that someone else had found these questions worthy of a thoughtful and thorough treatment.

35. Raïssa Maritain, *We Have Been Friends Together*, trans. Julie Kernan (New York: Longmans, Green, 1942), 72–78.

36. Augustine, *Confessions* 10.23.33. I was helped particularly in what follows (and on *curiositas* in general) by Stephen Menn's essay "The Desire for God and the Aporetic Method in Augustine's *Confessions*," in *Augustine's Confessions: Philosophy in Autobiography*, ed. W. E. Mann (Oxford: Oxford University Press, 2014), 72–107. My claim that Augustine does not mean to condemn the free play of the intellect by condemning *curiositas* is my own, and it is unusual; I do not know whether Menn would endorse it.

37. I am indebted to the wonderful discussion by Jean-Charles Nault, OSB, *The Noonday Devil: Acedia, the Unnamed Evil of Our Times* (San Francisco: Ignatius, 2013).

38. Thomas Aquinas, *On Evil*, trans. Jean Oesterle (Notre Dame, IN: University of Notre Dame Press, 1995), qu. 11, art. 4. Thomas cites Aristotle for the human inability to endure pain for long: see *Nicomachean Ethics* 8.6, 1158a23–24.

39. Elena Ferrante, *My Brilliant Friend*, trans. Ann Goldstein (New York: Europa, 2012), 47.

40. Ferrante, 79, 104, 119, 163, 198, 276.

41. Ferrante, 325.

42. Ferrante, 277.

43. Ferrante, 25.

44. Ferrante, 106.

45. Elena Ferrante, *The Story of a New Name*, trans. Ann Goldstein (New York: Europa, 2013), 15.

46. Elena Ferrante, *The Story of the Lost Child*, trans. Ann Goldstein (New York: Europa, 2015), 402–3.

47. Ferrante, *Story of a New Name*, 89.

48. Ferrante, *The Story of a New Name,* 443.

49. Elena Ferrante, *Those Who Leave and Those Who Stay*, trans. Ann Goldstein (New York: Europa, 2014), 53, my emphases.

50. Ferrante, *My Brilliant Friend*, 312.

51. Ferrante, *Story of a New Name*, 267.

52. Ferrante, *My Brilliant Friend*, 261.

Chapter 3

1. Ferrante, *Story of a New Name*, 133–34.

2. Ferrante, 162–63.

3. Ferrante, 409.

4. Ferrante, 409–10.

5. Petrement, "Year of Factory Work," 257.

6. Petrement, 258–59.

7. USA: Paramount, 1941. Versions of this section along with "The Use of the Inner World" (below, 185–187) and "Freedom and Aspiration" (below, 188–190) appeared in my essay "Why Intellectual Work Matters", *Modern Age*, Summer 2017.

8. I am indebted to an unpublished essay by Aline Gram on Dorothy Day's reading, through which I saw the relevance of Day to my work as well as the broad significance of reading for Day.

9. Robert Coles, introduction to *The Long Loneliness*, by Dorothy Day (San Francisco: HarperSanFrancisco, 1997), 4.

10. Dorothy Day, *From Union Square to Rome* (Maryknoll, NY: Orbis, 2006), 35.

11. Day, 37.

12. Day, 128–29.

13. Saint John of the Cross, *Living Flame of Love*, ed. and trans. E. Allison Peers (Garden City, NY: Image, 1962), sec. 17, 94–95.

14. Day, *From Union Square*, 4; cf. *Long Loneliness*, 255.

15. Day, *From Union Square*, 8.

16. Day, *From Union Square*, 8.

17. Day, *Long Loneliness*, 93.

18. Day, *From Union Square*, 125.

19. Day, *Long Loneliness*, 88.

20. Day, *From Union Square*, 18.

21. Quoted in Day, *From Union Square*, 94, 106; cf. *Long Loneliness*, 101–2.

22. Day, *From Union Square*, 11.

23. Day, *From Union Square*,140; *Long Loneliness*, 142.

24. William James, *The Varieties of Religious Experience* (New York: Library of America, 2009).

25. Quoted in Rose, *Intellectual Life*, 21.

26. Quoted in Rose, 54.

27. Albert Schweitzer, *Out of My Life and Thought* (New York: Henry Holt, 1949), 91–92.

28. Daniel David Luckenbill, *The Annals of Sennacherib* (Chicago: University of Chicago, 1924), 1. Luckenbill has less fortunate forms of grandiosity—say, about "oriental despotism" or "The East" in general—but the human questions can be appealed to without hackneyed or agenda-driven stereotyping.

29. So far as I know, Clooney did no such thing. I made this up (as I did the previous quote), and I mean him no harm by it.

30. See "Data Snapshot: Contingent Faculty in US Higher Ed," American Association of University Professors, n.d. (accessed June 3, 2019), https://www.aaup.org/sites/default/files/10112018%20Data%20Snapshot%20Tenure.pdf.

INDEX

academics/scholars: adjuncts, 200–201; diagnosis of contemporary, 199–200; disillusionment with the life of, 7, 11–12, 15–18; intellectual life and, 48. *See also* higher education

Achache, Mona, 54

Aeschylus, 85

Al-Asaad, Khaled, 43, 80

ambition: the danger of, 191; difficulty of circumstances and, 149–52; the love of learning and, 161; politics and, 165–69; the work of art and, 152–60

Ambrose (Archbishop of Milan), 60–61, 131, 140

Angelico, Giovanni, *Annunciation*, 60

Archimedes, 56–57, 63, 94, 115

Aristophanes, 117–23, 126, 188

Aristotle: on contemplation, 36, 44, 211n3; final end, distinguishing types of desire by, 31; highest good, seeking the, 32; the intellect as something divine, thinking of, 186; ultimate end, happiness as, 43; ultimate end, seeking, 35; virtues are learned by imitation, 196

Arnade, Chris, 215n51

Arnold, Matthew, 94

art: ambition and, 152–60; meaning of, 158–59

asceticism, 85–87, 93, 98, 113–14, 123

Ashbery, John, 41

Auden, W. H., 149

Augustine of Hippo, Saint: at the beginning of his search for wisdom, 189; believers are meant to hear, 63; *Confessions*, 72–74, 113, 117, 127–40, 148, 217n28; intellectual life, story about, 47; love and learning, relationship of, 110–11; love of spectacle, condemnation of, 132–41, 143; *On Order,* 136; redemption of, philosophical discipline and, 127–32; redemption of, the virtue of seriousness and, 144–48, 217n34; redemption of, truth and, 160–61

Austen, Jane, 86, 195

Autobiography of Malcolm X, 107–8

Baker, John, 40, 42, 78–80, 128

Barbery, Muriel, 127

Bembry, John Elton, 69

Bennet, Elizabeth, 96

Bennett, Arnold, 37

Bible, the, 1, 180–82

Blake, William, 124

Bloodworth, James, 38

Body Worlds, 134–35

books, Dorothy Day and, 176–79

Bourdieu, Pierre, 125

Cather, Willa, 86

Catholicism: author's entering, 14; Day's conversion to, 180–84

Cicero, 129, 152–53